DayDreaming

Martin,

Have a Happy Christmas and a fantastic 2014

Best Wishes

DayDreaming
SimonClarkson

THINKWORKS

For Laurie, Eve and Henry
– My Home

British Library Cataloguing in Publication Data:
A catalogue record of this book is available from The British Library.

ISBN 978-0-9574116-0-9

Design by Paul Airy of DesignLeft
www.designleft.co.uk

Printed and bound in the United Kingdom by Bell & Bain, Glasgow.

13   Introduction
25   Luck
37   Dreams or Reality

49   The Rules
53   Rule One **Make It Personal**
67   Rule Two **There Is No Time Like The Present**

77   **Wayne Howard**

95   Rule Three **The Devil Is In The Detail**
109   Rule Four **Give Yourself Goose Bumps**

117   **Mike Mair**

129   Rule Five **Don't Look Now But...**
141   Rule Six **Nothing Compares To You**

151   **Nick Shakibai**

165   Rule Seven **You Can't Kid A Kidder**
181   Rule Eight **A Need To Know Basis**

191   **Neil Osgood**

203   Rule Nine **Walk The Tightrope**
213   Rule Ten **The Pen Is Mightier...**

221   **Jan Rhodes**

237   Rule Eleven **The Prescription**

247   DayDreaming
252   Books
254   Thanks

Contents

"All men dream, but not equally. Those who dream by night in the dusty recesses of their minds wake in the day to find that it was vanity: but the dreamers of the day are dangerous men, for they may act their dreams with open eyes, to make it possible."

T. E. LAWRENCE, THE SEVEN PILLARS OF WISDOM

Introduction

What makes a retiree decide to go out and use his new found freedom to achieve perhaps the most audacious goal he had ever set? How does someone achieve a lifelong dream, when most people might believe it is not realistically possible to do so? Why does a person who 'settled' all his life for a safe career, drop everything and go and chase his passion? How does someone who has developed a severe phobia overcome it? What is it that drives a person to eventually find success in something that they have failed to overcome their entire life?

One thing is for sure, none of the above are ever done on a whim!

Why is it that some people achieve when others don't? Why is it that some people seem to 'get things done', whilst others procrastinate and never 'get round to it'? Why do some people spend their lives wishing and hoping, whereas others take action? This book contains the answer; it is simple and it applies to everyone and any goal. We will explore this simple answer alongside 5 main case studies and many real life examples.

We dream about achieving things everyday. The problem is that those dreams often remain just that…dreams. Everyone has the ability to turn their dreams into reality. Whether we do it big or small, DayDreaming, when we do it properly, is the only reason we ever achieve anything at all.

If this scares you, put this book down. If this intrigues you, read on.

Did you know that one of the world's most successful and revered film makers was refused a loan of $20,000 in order to make his first film? If you think about the facts, he had a lot going against him:

- An untried and untested idea – it had never been done before to the extent that he wanted to
- An idea that required artistic skills that he didn't posses – his friend was the talented artist
- No security to offer in exchange for the loan – at the time he rented a small flat and had no savings
- A less than respectable credit rating – twice before he had been declared bankrupt

No wonder they laughed him out of the bank. Many people would think he was crazy to even bother asking. In fact, he was laughed out of over 300 banks before he finally heard the word he needed: yes.

 ## "If you can dream it, you can do it."
WALT DISNEY

Disney became one of the best-known motion picture producers in the world, as well as an innovator in animation and theme park design. He holds the record for the individual with the most Oscar wins and the most nominations.

What Mr Disney had more than any other was a formula for success, a blueprint that he followed. He was no more intelligent, richer or luckier than anyone else. He just knew a few simple things and applied them. These simple things we apply everyday of our lives but don't realise it. Let me demonstrate.

Have a good, long think about what you are going to eat
for your next meal. Take your time. Whether it is breakfast lunch
or dinner, picture it in your mind's eye. Picture it clearly, see
not just the meal but the room you are in, your surroundings,
the plate, the table if appropriate. Hear the noises around you,
smell the food, look around the picture in all its detailed, 'Techni-
colour' glory. Add realism to the picture. Think about what you
really do want and really do believe you could have.

I am sure that as you pictured your meal, you most likely
saw it sat on your plate, perhaps on your dining table, possibly in
a restaurant or on your knee in front of the television; or maybe
still in the pan or the oven, waiting to be served from the stove;
you might have even imagined lifting a forkful to your mouth,
practically tasting the food as you bite and chew.

Congratulations. You have just set a goal; a small and
perhaps relatively insignificant goal, but a goal all the same. You
have just used your amazing power of imagination. You have
actually just built a physical pathway, hardwiring your brain and
creating a connection that provides a route for you to follow
and achieve that very goal. Like a road being laid, a wire being
connected, a channel being cut, you have just given yourself a
path to follow to the destination. You have awoken an area of
your brain that will now filter in the opportunities that constantly
surround you in order to achieve that goal. You have just truly
DayDreamed. The more you picture this DayDream, the more
you will behave towards it and turn it into reality.

We are truly brilliant at setting goals. Often these are for smaller things that we consider to be insignificant. We carry out the process many times everyday of our lives. However, when it comes to bigger dreams, more audacious goals, we lose sight of the target itself and hold ourselves back by using our imagination in a negative way; by thinking about all the potential problems and barriers that could get in our way. We stop really DayDreaming.

The truth is we set goals all the time.

It doesn't matter that the majority of these goals are compromises, or scaled down versions of what we really would like. If you picture yourself ending up in the same job, in the same house, eating the same food, earning the same money, then you are still setting goals. You are still DayDreaming. You are just DayDreaming for the same old stuff. The other, brighter, more attractive goals remain just dreams; stuff of fantasy.

From what we will have for dinner, to the route we will take home from work; from where we will go on holiday this year to which television programmes we intend to watch this week. We cannot escape the inevitable truth that is goal setting. It is the way we are put together.

 "You won't get anything unless you have the vision to imagine it."
JOHN LENNON

18

Why then, when we are so well practised at using this amazingly powerful tool, do we regularly fail to use it to its true potential?

Take a piece of paper (half a sheet of A4 will work great) and write on it in large bold letters the word 'PROBLEMS'. On another sheet of paper write in big bold letters the word 'GOAL' and place that a few metres away from you, propping it up so you can see the word. Step back a few paces and hold the paper with 'PROBLEMS' written on it about half an arm's length away so that you can see the word 'GOAL' in the distance just over the top of it.

Focus on the word 'GOAL'. When we focus on the goal we have clarity of purpose. We give our brain the signal it needs in order drive our behaviour accordingly, with passion, energy, determination and more. We give ourselves the very best chance of achieving the goal.

Now, without moving the paper, just cast your eyes a little lower and focus on the word 'PROBLEMS'. Notice on the far sheet, the word 'GOAL' blurs out of focus. When we start to focus on the problems, the goal becomes difficult to see or blurs out of our vision altogether.

When you focus on the hurdles as opposed to the finish line, they may just dominate the horizon.

With larger goals, goals that we perceive may have more of these barriers blocking our path, we often focus on all of the problems instead of what it is that we really want out of it. We need to get our minds on the 'DayDream' behind the goal, rather than on everything that will get in the way.

Randy Pausch, a man who knowingly had to give his 'final lecture' to students after being diagnosed as terminally ill said; "Walls aren't there to keep you out; they are there so you can prove how much you want something."

Let's start to knock the walls down.

 "The future belongs to those who believe in the beauty of their dreams."
ELEANOR ROOSEVELT

Every book has flaws. This one is no different. If you read it trying to find them then I have no doubt you will be successful. In writing it to suit as wide a group as possible, I will probably over simplify for some people's taste, and over complicate for others'. If you read it trying to find the potential, I am sure you will.

This book is two things.

It is a journal containing a handful of amazing stories of people who have achieved against the odds, of people that dived headfirst into their dreams and made them a reality.

It is also an education as to HOW they did it. As we explore their stories, you will discover the really simple rules of working with your imagination to make it work for you. It is not an 'academic' book, yet all of these rules are well researched, well founded and well proven.

I will describe these rules and give countless examples of people who have applied them to achieve goals whether they are:

- **Big or small**
- **Everyday or once in a lifetime**
- **Work or play**
- **Long term or short term**
- **Group or individual**

"The real secret of success is that there is no secret!"

W. CLEMENT STONE

Luck

I am a firm believer that you make your own luck in life; that we are *drivers* of our fate, not *passengers*. Even I have to admit though, there was an unsettlingly significant level of 'chance' about my working in the field of personal and organisational development.

I had just returned from a year long honeymoon with my wife (of course!), a little earlier than originally planned, with no home, no money and scariest of all, no plan. After trading for a large investment bank in London for five years, I had decided it was time to return home to the North West. Laurie and I tied the knot and travelled around the world for a year, as much to avoid the question of what we were going to do when we 'grew up', as to see something of it.

My parents picked us up from the airport and I can still remember to this day asking them as we passed over the Thelwall Viaduct near Warrington; "Do you want to take us out for dinner so we can tell you about our trip?" We wanted to share our exciting stories but didn't have the money to buy the meal! My parents, guilt ridden looks on their faces, apologised profusely, stating some 'charity ball' they couldn't get out of.

Great! Their only son, returned home after a year and they couldn't even organise their diary to be with him and their new daughter-in-law on their first night home.

As it turned out, I am glad they couldn't. After a tipsy conversation (or two) at that very same charity ball, my loving mother had organised my first interview. The rest is history. Within half an hour, I knew that this was to become my life; 'changing people's lives' has a nice ring to it don't you think? 10 years on, it now seems strange to think that I could have ended up doing anything else.

If it hadn't been for my mother, perhaps I would never have had the opportunity. Yet given what I have learnt so far, I am convinced the opportunity would have arisen from elsewhere if not then. Perhaps my mother was just the catalyst.

Either way, being honest with myself, that 'chance meeting' wasn't the only factor.

- **I had to make the call**
- **I had to make the right first impression**
- **I had to go through a *rigorous* three month interview process**
- **I had to chase and chase what quickly became, as W. Clement Stone once said, an *'all consuming dream'***
- **I even had to work for free to prove my worth!!!**
- **I had to *use* my lucky break**

Since then there have been numerous challenges along the way that I have had to deal with. It has been anything but easy. However, without ALL of those challenges and without that first introduction into this world, Think Works would not exist today.

I guess therefore you could say that luck is something to be taken advantage of, rather than something to be relied upon. Perhaps luck does exist, but my experience of the last six years, and the amazing people that I work with day in day out, is that luck is useless unless someone uses it. Luck needs taking advantage of.

Luck is a state of mind. I was driving home one evening when I saw motorway signs flash up the news of an accident ahead and the delays that had been caused. 'Unlucky people' would spend the next ten minutes cursing their lot in life as they joined the back of the queue. 'Lucky people' find consolation in the fact that they were warned about the delay and were able to take 'evasive action'. If they can't even do that, 'lucky people' will tell themselves that this is an opportunity to listen to music, or make those phone calls (hands free of course!) to family they have been meaning to make for a few weeks. 'Unlucky people' will moan about that time it took. 'Lucky people' will be happy they weren't ten minutes earlier as it could have been them at the bottom of the pile of cars. Perhaps luck is a choice?

Dr. Richard Wiseman carried out a fascinating experiment during extensive research on the phenomenon of luck. He gave a newspaper to a group of people; some of whom perceived themselves as lucky and some unlucky, and asked them to look through it recording how many photographs were inside. He secretly placed a large message halfway through the newspaper saying: "Tell the experimenter you have seen this and win £250."

This message took up half of the page and was written in type that was more than two inches high. Statistically, the results showed that those who considered themselves unlucky tended to miss the advertisement and those that considered themselves lucky tended to see it.

A good friend of mine bought some shelves at Ikea, only to find that the shelves were too long for the alcove they were destined for. He decided (some would say foolishly) to take them back on a Bank Holiday Monday. Everyone knows what Ikea is like on a Bank Holiday! He walked into the returns area to find a long queue of people waiting to be served. He noticed there was a machine where you take a ticket with a number to give you your turn. Unlucky people may look at the queue, think 'no way' and turn around cursing their 'luck'. He patiently got his ticket and took his place at the back of the line, even though he was on a tight schedule. The P.A. system announced the next number as "241". He looked at his ticket. It read "242". He looked around, confused that he would therefore be called up next, seeing only then the other, even more confused faces around him. Everyone in the line had missed the machine. As they all then ran to get the next number, he stepped forward to the front of the queue thinking; "how lucky am I?!"

Lucky people are only lucky because they *think* they are lucky. By thinking they are lucky a particular area within their brain kicks into action and begins to spot opportunities for *luck*. This particular area is called the Reticular Activating Cortex, which acts as a filter, allowing certain information through and blocking the rest out.

Have you ever bought a car and then noticed something strange?

It suddenly seems as though everyone else has the same car...they are everywhere!

Of course, you know and I know that those cars were on the road before you started taking an interest but you never actually *saw* them before. You are exposed to trillions of pieces of information like this on a daily basis. You need to sort which information is relevant and which isn't. This is your filter, your

Reticular Activating Cortex, working overtime. This incredibly sensitive, hugely powerful and frighteningly relentless part of your grey matter is responsible for everything you ever *notice* or indeed everything that ever *passes you by*. The beauty of it is that YOU tell it what to allow in and what to block out. Therefore; I say it again. Lucky people are those that think lucky – those that wake their brain up and filter in the opportunities that surround us all.

And so it is with goals. From what we will have for dinner, to climbing Everest; when we set goals properly, focusing on the right things, we wake up this amazing part of our brain and this incredible talent we have for spotting the opportunities around us. When we set goals improperly and focus on the wrong things, we set our filter up to spot all the hurdles rather than the finish line. Set a DayDream and suddenly you will start noticing all the signs that point to the destination.

There is luck everywhere. To be lucky however, you need a brain tuned into the right frequency to pick it up. This reminds me of a great story about the South African golfer Gary Player. He was practising bunker shots as a teenager at his local club when two senior members walked past. He holed a shot straight from the sand and they saw it happen. The men were amazed and bet that he couldn't do it again. Player threw three balls down into the sand and holed his second shot! "That was lucky" cried one of the men.

"Sir, the more I practise, the luckier I get" said Player.

How many ideas do you ever have that don't make it past the start line? More often than not, the reason why they don't is because we don't believe they will. We may tell ourselves "there is no point" or "that the risks are too big." What if James Dyson had said that before he spent 5 years producing 5127 prototypes before the world's first bagless vacuum cleaner finally made it to market? Was he lucky? Maybe: was he prepared to keep going when others may have quit? Definitely: did he make his own luck? I certainly think so.

True DayDreaming is a methodology you have used everyday since you were born, in order to achieve things big or small – in order to cut your own slice of luck and achieve positive outcomes. All this book intends to do is to show you how you do it, so that you can use it more often and for bigger and even better things. This book will show you the difference between day dreaming as we think it is, and DayDreaming as we would wish it to be, bringing our fantasies into reality. How do we make sure that that we are 'lucky' more often?

"Yes, it's true; luck does play a part in it. But if you believe, and are determined, you can build your own luck…and realise that vision is really not so far away"

ELLEN MACARTHUR

Dreams or Reality

"I have a dream."

These words were made famous by Martin Luther King in Washington DC on August 28th 1963, whilst standing on the steps of the Lincoln Memorial. This was where more than 250,000 people (20% of whom were white) gathered to hear what was rumoured to have been prepared by King as a fairly short and plain rendition of the suffering faced by Black Americans at that time.

A gospel singer, Mahalia Jackson, shouted out from the crowd; "Tell them about your dream, Martin! Tell them about the dream!" And so he did.

It was his homage to this **dream** that made the speech so powerful and ultimately memorable. He didn't describe a simple goal. He described what the end result of that goal would be. He described, as Jackson had begged, his ***dream;*** a **dream** of all people, no matter their colour, living in a free and just America. The speech became a watershed in the civil rights movement in America.

*"I say to you today, my friends, so even though we face the difficulties of today and tomorrow, I still have a **dream**. It is a **dream** deeply rooted in the American **dream**.*

*I have a **dream** that one day this nation will rise up and live out the true meaning of its creed: We hold these truths to be self-evident: that all men are created equal.*

*I have a **dream** that one day on the red hills of Georgia the sons of former slaves and the sons of former slave owners will be able to sit down together at the table of brotherhood.*

*I have a **dream** that one day even the state of Mississippi, a state sweltering with the heat of injustice, sweltering with the heat of oppression, will be transformed into an oasis of freedom and justice.*

*I have a **dream** that my four little children
will one day live in a nation where they will not be
judged by the colour of their skin but by the content
of their character.*

*I have a **dream** today.*

*I have a **dream** that one day, down in
Alabama, with its vicious racists, with its governor
having his lips dripping with the words of
interposition and nullification; one day right there in
Alabama, little black boys and black girls will be able
to join hands with little white boys and white girls as
sisters and brothers.*

*I have a **dream** today.*

*I have a **dream** that one day every valley shall
be exalted, every hill and mountain shall be made
low, the rough places will be made plain, and the
crooked places will be made straight, and the glory
of the Lord shall be revealed, and all flesh shall see
it together."*

MARTIN LUTHER KING

It is this DayDreaming that drives and indeed enables
us to achieve. It is this process, which we all know how to
use, and have used it countless times in the past, that makes
achievement of any size, shape or type possible.

The interesting thing is King's ability to separate the *goal* from the *dream*. The goal was to forward the cause of the civil rights movement in America. The dream was more than that. It was the picture, the passion and the vision behind the goal. It was this dream that helped to pave the way for the election of America's first black president, Barrack Obama. People dreamt about the possibility, building their belief in the probability, in order to behave in such a way that made it an inevitability.

My good friend and colleague Heather once summed this up brilliantly by asking the question; what did Martin Luther King say he had?

Was it?

A: I have a SMART goal
B: I have a Personal Development Plan
C: I have a *dream*

This is about bringing your goals to *LIFE!*

Read it again and *feel* King's words. Picture King standing there and saying it; do you feel the shivers down your spine?

The DayDream is the ideal state, the point when you know you have achieved the goal, that picture or vision of the goal itself.

This is where visualisation comes from.

Visualisation is something that is often talked about as magical and mysterious, even verging on ridiculous. This is by those who understand neither the process nor the reasons for it. It is perceived as something that only high performers, such as elite sports people or self made millionaires, do. Is it any wonder why these people, who admit to using visualisation extensively, appear to achieve goals that others believe to be beyond their grasp? This is no coincidence.

See this example from Gordon Ramsey's autobiography which I recently read. He describes a time in his life where he worked as Head Chef on a multi-millionaire's boat.

*"If you were a certain kind of guy, you would wait till you were out of your uniform and your employer was on dry land, and then you'd pass the boat off as your own… I think some of the deck hands started to believe their own fantasies in the end – they'd lived the lifestyle for too long… But not me. **I kept my imaginary restaurant – my dream – in my mind's eye at all times. I never let myself forget that this, for me, was just another leg in my journey. And I could feel myself getting closer to achieving it every day. I could almost SMELL that restaurant of mine. It was in my sights."***

Visualisation is something that we all do all the time. As demonstrated previously, your ability to 'picture' your goals is the very thing that enables you to achieve any of them, small or large. Most self-help books do indeed tell us this very fact. I didn't invent it. If anyone tries to tell you this is new, you know that they are either mistaken, or are lying. A friend of mine, Damian, writes fantastic books on this very subject and he hits the nail on the head by quoting Isaac Newton: "If I have seen a little farther it is by standing on the shoulders of giants."

Visualisation, or DayDreaming as I describe the process here, is where all success originates from.

Think about any skill you mastered as a child. Catching a ball or riding a bike. The first thing we do is *watch* someone else do it. Then we start to picture ourselves doing that very same thing. The cognitive process we go through is the equivalent to creating a blueprint for the process itself. Of course, like a building, the blueprint needs physical work to make it a reality. However, you would never build anything without first having that blueprint.

These blueprints are nothing more than physical connections in your brain. Connections formed by an electrical impulse, set off by a thought, allowing chemical information to be transferred. The process of thinking about something, picturing or visualising it, builds that pathway in your brain. That same pathway you have built in the 'thinking' is then used in the 'doing'.

The truth is, on some levels, your brain doesn't know the difference between something you visualise or imagine and something you are actually doing in reality. Have you ever watched someone playing a games console? They physically move with the game even though they are not actually racing or fighting a real car or opponent. They are playing a game which constructs an imaginary scenario and their heart rate physically rises! The same happens when you watch an exciting event – I feel tired after watching a game of rugby on the television. My wife laughs at how I move, push and twitch around in sympathy with the players during the game! Thoughts build real pathways in the brain. Those pathways are responsible for our behavioural patterns. That is why people feel sick when they 'think' of a food or drink that they cannot stand. It's why people get scared in haunted houses; even though they 'know' deep down that this is just a theme park!

Have you ever heard the phrase 'practice makes perfect?' Well this is true, in that the more times you use a pathway in your brain, through thought or action, the 'stronger' that pathway becomes. Think of this as **'bandwidth'** on an internet connection; the stronger the connection is, the faster the flow of information. Therefore, if the pathways we use to 'do' things are the same as those with which we 'think' about doing things, then we must come to the following conclusion:

Every thought you have, hardwires your brain to produce the behaviour you think about.

There have been many studies done on the power of visualisation. One involved a US College basketball squad splitting themselves into two teams of equal ability (as far as their individual averages would allow). They would have a 'throw off' from the penalty line. Half the team warmed up out on the court, taking practise shots. Half the team warmed up by thinking about taking penalty shots. The team that visualised their shots first won… easily. In fact, the more they did this, the more they won by. Why do you think this happened? The team that practised out on court missed shots during their warm up too. They *practised imperfectly*. The team that spent time visualising their shots *practised perfectly*. During THEIR visualised warm up session, how many do you think they missed? Zero. Only Homer Simpson misses in his mind!

We must understand that 'practice still makes perfect' even when we practice imperfectly. We simply perfect the very thing we are doing incorrectly. In other words, we become better at doing things badly if that is the way we practice them. The true phrase should therefore be 'practice makes **permanent**.'

The only way to begin to practice something perfectly is if you can visualise it perfectly first. This builds the connection in your brain, which you then use again in physical practice and ultimately in performing the task: as long as you have created good enough bandwidth. Perfection therefore comes as a result of 'perfect practice'. Perfect practice could only come as a result of perfect visualisation.

Now for the 64 thousand dollar question: What is good enough bandwidth? Simple; it is that which gives you no option other than to use it. These connections, created by your thoughts and actions, begin as charges of electricity that allow chemicals to move between one brain cell and another.

Remember, the more times you use a pathway, the greater the bandwidth – the less resistance there is to the information flowing down that route again. Electricity always travels down the path of least resistance. Even I can remember that from school! Therefore, the more times you use a pathway the better chance you have of creating one that you physically have no choice but to use again and again. This is why people form habits. This is why behaviours become automatic and subconscious. Have you ever moved house and subsequently driven part way to your previous address before realising where you are? Repetition breeds the likelihood of further repetition.

As I have already mentioned, these charges of electricity allow a chemical transfer to take place along the pathway itself. Significantly for us, the amount of chemicals transferred is within our control. These chemicals, at their most basic, are our emotions and physical drivers. The more emotion we involve in the process, the larger the amount of chemicals will be transferred. The more emotion, the bigger the physical drive to behave accordingly. It isn't just how many times we visualise something therefore; it is how powerfully we visualise it – how much emotion is involved.

We build these blueprints in our brain through intensity as well as frequency of thought.

Intensity x Frequency = Bandwidth

$$I \times F = B$$

This is why many people give up smoking after a major health scare for example. The intensity of the experience builds greater bandwidth in a shorter time.

With each thought you have, you are increasing the probability, to a varying degree, that you will automatically come to use this pathway or blueprint in reality. The stronger we draw our blueprint, the stronger the likelihood of success.

When used correctly, your vision becomes more than just a fantasy. This becomes a DayDream and you will, in turn, make it a reality. These blueprints really do become our pathways to success.

"I never hit a shot, not even in practice, without having a very sharp, in-focus picture of it in my head. It's like a colour movie. First I see the ball where I want it to finish, nice and white and sitting up high on bright green grass."

JACK NICKLAUS

The Rules

How do you turn a goal into a DayDream?

What really brings it to life?

What turns a fantasy into a process that drives your behaviours towards making it a reality?

How do I ensure that I create the correct picture, to build the RIGHT pathway in my brain that will WORK for me?

Over the remainder of the book you will discover the simple rules that will enable you to apply this process to any goal. These eleven rules will demonstrate, step by step, how to construct these DayDreams. How to conceive them, write them and what to do next with them.

In between those rules sit the incredible stories of people who have applied these simple rules and turned their goals into DayDreams. They have simply turned their fantasies into reality. There are also a series of exercises to give you some practice at constructing your own.

You can read the rest of this book any way it suits you; as written, or rules together followed by the stories later. You can complete the exercises as you go, or leave them until the end.

Most importantly, grab a pen and make it yours.

Underline, circle, take notes and start building your DayDreams.

"You can't depend on your eyes when your imagination is out of focus."

MARK TWAIN

RuleOne
MakeIt
Personal

1

It's YOUR goal.

You can start by painting *your* picture of your dream in the first person. Emphasise *your* involvement in that picture.

Some people talk about watching themselves as if on a television screen. Go further than that. This is more than just watching yourself in the third person, more than just seeing yourself *doing* it from the outside looking in. This is 'living it' in your mind, *being* it. Remember, we are human *beings* not human *doings*. Adrian Gilpin called this process of visualisation 'Dreaming Awake'. Rather than seeing yourself as if removed from your body, look at it from your own perspective; see it from your own eyes.

This is YOUR dream. Not anyone else's. The first step to individualisation of a goal is to think about it from your perspective. Your description of this dream must take place in the first person. The word "I" should therefore appear a great deal.

As you will see, this subject of individualisation crops up numerous times. A person's interpretation of the goal is exactly what DayDreaming is truly about. Any drab sounding goal can be turned into any number of individual, personalised, emotive pictures or visions. The picture must be the one that you find most inspiring, the one that is most personal to you. The very process of turning the goal into your picture should result in a degree of personalisation anyway.

DayDreaming has no ultimate 'right' answer. There are ways and means of arriving at your picture, but the end result is yours and yours alone.

Example: **A Family**

I am not usually in the business of telling all my personal secrets. I think it is better to talk of others' achievements than one's own. However, this example comes straight from the heart. My wife and I had always wanted to have a family. However, 1 year after we decided to try, we had not had a glimmer of success. We began to worry as anyone would. I had my DayDream to keep me strong.

The goal was to have a family.

My DayDream was as follows:

I am stood looking at my wife and newborn child as they meet for the first time. We are in the hospital and everything is calm after the storm. A smile stretches across my face that I have been waiting to show the world for 9 months. I whisper to Laurie that I will be back in 30 seconds and turn to walk to the door of the delivery room. This is the moment that I have been looking forward to. I push the door open and turn to face my Mum and Dad outside in the hall. The smile is still there as I utter the words; "It's a …!"

Although the goal involves others, it is still written about me and my experience of the event. It is written in the first person. It is still written from my perspective. This makes the DayDream mine. The goal is OUR goal. The picture is mine.

My wife's picture was very different. Her vision was more focused on being at home with the baby after the birth, which she of course saw as a 'task' to achieve the goal. She had it all worked out in her head. Her picture was different to mine, even though the goal was the same.

This just demonstrates that everybody's picture should be individual to them. There is no one vision for a particular goal.

I must emphasise here that there are, of course, sometimes things that are simply physically impossible to do. No amount of DayDreaming would create a baby if I were infertile. However, DayDreaming, if carried through properly, would drive me to continue in my quest for a family through other means if I found out that were the case.

The above example of DayDreaming demonstrates the ability to develop truly effective goals that involve more than one person e.g. a team goal, family goal or even an organisational goal. The goal can be the same even though everyone's DayDream or picture of that goal is different. The very fact that your picture must be personalised allows people to make a joint goal individual to them; they can internalise it and engage with it. This process allows individuals to find the personal vision that will drive *their* behaviours towards it. If a critical mass of people in that group delivers on their part, this gives the very best chance of achieving that overall goal.

Every goal has infinite possibilities behind it. Everyone could describe their own picture. Every picture would be different – allowing teams to generate individual buy in to a shared goal, and organisations to generate individual buy in to a shared vision. In fact this is exactly how organisations should 'roll out' their overall vision and goals.

Example: **Promotion**

In the work we carried out a few years ago with Bolton Wanderers we spent time with all staff (players included), helping them to set goals. The ultimate goal at that time was promotion into the Premier League. The beauty was that from the receptionist to the chairman, from star player to boot boy, everyone in the club was able to form their own DayDream as to what that goal meant to them. This helps each individual 'buy into' the goal and gives them a personal vision to drive them.

Here are just a couple, written in short form, that give an idea for the variety, given different people's positions within the organisation. There are not all exactly as the individuals wrote them, but they should give you a good idea.

It is September 2000 and I am stepping out onto the turf at Highbury (Arsenal's ground). This is our third game of the season and the one I have been looking forward to all along. I look up into the crowd and see my wife and son waving proudly as I hear the crowd roar to greet the home team. The Bolton fans in the far corner cheer their first visit to a premier league stadium for a few years. Back where I belong, on the big stage, and my son will remember seeing his dad on this day for the rest of his life!

It is August 2000 and I am walking through the chairman's lounge at the Reebok Stadium (Bolton's ground) serving drinks. It's been a fantastic day as I have just seen Bolton's return to the big time and I was a part of it! I turn and brush shoulders with someone who I immediately recognise. My boyhood hero; Ian Rush, walks right by me. I really am rubbing shoulders with the stars!

It doesn't matter what role these two individuals play within the club. They both need to buy into the goal and, by painting their very own picture, this way they can.

Bolton went on to gain promotion that season. Over the next few seasons they 'over achieved' time and time again according to the press and pundits. They did not 'over achieve' according to their well formed DayDreams.

Whether it is a team, family, organisation or indeed an individual goal, the picture must be personal to you.

TopTips

- **Form your picture of the goal; make it personal**
- **'Live' your goal – don't just see it happening**
- **Use the words I or me in the description to ensure YOUR involvement**
- **For group DayDreams allow everyone to form their OWN picture to drive them**

Every goal has an infinite number of pictures behind it. Below are three simplified examples. I have taken three goals and then given MY personalised version of the DayDream behind that goal; the picture in my mind that would show me what it would be like when I achieve the goal. I have kept them short and sweet for the moment.

The goal: To buy a house by the sea.

The dream: I am walking out of my front door, the sun shining, the sound of seagulls flying overhead, interrupting the gentle lapping of waves against the pebble beach.

The goal: To win a tennis match.

The dream: I step up to the net to shake hands with my crestfallen opponent, hot and sweaty, exhausted but satisfied, thinking how much I deserve that cool beer in the bar afterwards.

The goal: To give a great wedding speech

The dream: I raise the glass of champagne, toast the bride and groom, catch a wink from my wife as she gives me the thumbs up and I know they loved it! I can relax now and enjoy the night.

Now it's your turn. Have a look at the following examples. They may not be your goals but describe

Exercise: Create your picture

your picture for each of them. It doesn't matter what path you take with the DayDream. At what point do YOU know YOU have got there? Express it in the first person.

The goal: To buy your dream car
The dream:

The goal: To reach a desired weight
The dream:

The goal: To learn a language
The dream:

Exercise: **Create your picture**

As you think about the dream, pictures should flash into your mind's eye. These pictures are you visualising your success. Try to live in this picture if you can. Now try this below with a couple of your own goals. Turn them into a picture and start to create a daydream for each.

Exercise: **Create your picture**

Exercise: **Create your picture**

"Imagination is the beginning of creation. You imagine what you desire, you will what you imagine and at last you create what you will."

THOMAS A. EDISON

RuleTwo
ThereIsNoTime LikeThePresent

2

Express your DayDream in the present tense.

Your brain works in the present tense. When you visualise anything, whether a dream about your future or indeed a memory of the past, you picture it in real time. You are trying to create pathways that drive behaviours NOW. Live in it, as if it is happening now.

Your imagination is a tool you have used many times in the past. You picture your wildest dreams in the same way that you picture your memories. AS THEY HAPPEN.

Ultimately you are trying to give your brain a destination to reach; the achievement of your goal. That destination is only reached through your behaviour. Those behaviours are needed NOW. You need to open up your filter to the opportunities that present themselves to help you achieve your goal as they happen.

It is very easy to feel comfortable by allowing your brain to imagine your achievements in the future. The future never comes. Tomorrow never comes. I could ALWAYS be rich next year. I could ALWAYS be organised next week. Persistently talking about the future may persistently keep it in the future. To get on with doing it now; that is the key. Even if the step is small, like writing this book. One page at a time. My dream of seeing it in real time on Amazon drives me to do it now, to behave NOW.

Even though you express this in the present tense, you should put a future date on it.

Of course! Logically you know that even though you are picturing this happening now, building pathways in your brain to drive your behaviours, you also know that this NOW is actually a future NOW. Muhammad Ali uses the phrase *'future history'*. He visualised his future as his history.

He publicly predicted the round he would win in 19 times and 17 of those he was correct. Later he was to keep his predictions secret from the press. They vilified him on the rare occasions he didn't achieve his vision. Rather than reporting the 17 correct predictions, they focused on the 2!

A date gives you a target point, when that NOW will actually take place. The really sharp ones reading this book will have noticed that in my example of starting a family previously, there was no date. There may be a few goals for which it is more difficult to put an actual date on. This is perhaps because you want to achieve it as soon as possible. In this case, as I have done, the date can be implied. I have implied it as 9 months hence in my DayDream (a realistic target for the length of a pregnancy as I understand it!). That way, the date rolls forward with each day that passes and continues to drive you towards your dream. Obviously, the longer it takes for progress to be made, the stronger you have to be in maintaining the DayDream in order to maintain your drive and commitment to the goal.

Where you can give yourself a date, do. This gives your brain a target to aim for. Your resulting behaviours will drive towards that date.

Example: **A second home**

My father, of all people, attended a programme that I
ran. Now, teaching people about their true potential, raising
their awareness of what holds them back and equipping them
to realise more of that potential is an awesome responsibility.
However, when your father is in the room and the student
becomes teacher to the teacher who becomes student, the
situation feels a little strange to say the least.

One of the dreams my father had had for a long time was
to own a house abroad. He had previously made forays into
buying apartments and renting them out, but he really wanted
a haven for him and his family; a place he could be proud of; a
little piece of private heaven.

The goal was therefore not just to own a property abroad,
but to own a home from home.

The DayDream he created in 2005 in order to drive him
towards the goal was as follows.

*It is summer 2006 and I am lying in the back garden of
our new Spanish house. I have my shades on and the stereo
is playing Billy Joel out onto the veranda. The sun burns down
on me and I feel the warmth spread through my body as sleep
threatens to envelop me. This is perfection! Palms in the corner
of the garden sway gently in the warm wind from the Sahara.*

I can hear little Grace giggling as she peers over the edge of the swimming pool – MY swimming pool! I feel a few drops of water on the soles of my feet and realise she is squirting me with her water pistol. I pretend not to notice and then, as she improves her aim and jets of water rain in on me, I jump up and ROAR! I jump over Grace and into the pool, and resurface to see Grace throwing her head backwards in uncontrollable fits of laughter. This is the life.

That dream drove him to do everything he needed to do in order to get there. The amount of inconvenience, time, effort, and most importantly to him, money that he had to part with in order to realise this dream was astonishing. However, at no point along that road did he waver, at least not outwardly. From the moment that his brain spotted the opportunity to buy in a beautiful village up in the hills of Lanzarote (how many times do you drive past 'for sale' signs without really noticing them, until it becomes important to you!?) to the three days he spent dismantling the oven, cleaning it and rebuilding it like new. His DayDream drove him forward. It continues to this day, despite the fact that little Grace has drenched him plenty of times from that pool now!

Don't just put it off. Build the right pathways to drive behaviours now. See it as if in a crystal ball. Put it in the present tense.

TopTips

- **Express the DayDream as if it is happening now**
- **Put a date on it to give you a target**
- **Imply a date if it is impossible to predict when you can achieve this**

"Champions aren't made in the gyms. Champions are made from something they have deep inside them – a desire, a dream, a vision."

MUHAMMAD ALI

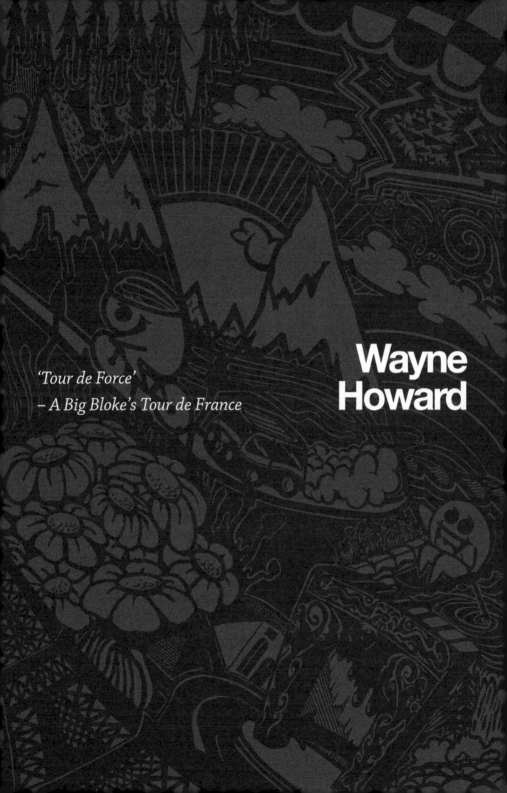

'Tour de Force'
– A Big Bloke's Tour de France

Wayne
Howard

I was one year away from completing 30 years Police service in
the Lancashire Constabulary and planned to retire from the service and
take my pension. I intended to then take full advantage of a window in
my life to attempt a major challenge, something that would seriously test
me, both to my physical and mental limits. I had competed as a veteran
in the sport of Indoor Rowing all over the world, and won lots of gold
medals, but I wanted to succeed in a new and completely different type
of enterprise; something I could look back upon with definitive pride. It's
great to live life well, but I wanted to have something major to look back
on and say – wow, I really did do that!

I was exploring the idea of different challenges; for example,
walking around Britain or Lands End to John O'Groats, but I have a back
problem and needed something that my body would hold up to. I'd always
steered away from cycling but Julie, my wife, bought me a book called
'French Revolutions' by Tim Moore, which is brilliantly funny, about
an ordinary bloke, a sports journalist from the Daily Telegraph, who
wanted to ride the 2000 Tour de France route. It is his diary of his 2,250
mile trek around France, and the world's toughest cycle race route. Julie
bought it because she knows I love sport and I read it in about 2 days!
However, just after I had put the book down, a thought started creeping
up on me – how great it would be for me to do it – so I looked up and said
to Julie, "that's it, I'm going to cycle the Tour de France!"

Julie's first response was to point out that I didn't even have a
bike! However, knowing me as an obsessive person whom once he sets
his mind to something he just has to do it, she simply said "OK, do it".
Bearing in mind that I had never really cycled, I obviously had no concept

as to quite how tough this would be. I just believed it was something I
could do and, even though I had no frame of reference for the enormity
of the challenge that lay ahead of me, my self belief was rock solid.
I just knew I could do it. I was going to do it properly, not ride around the
Pyrenees and Alps like Tim Moore did, which is impressive enough, but
actually ride over them, doing the entire route – It would be interesting
to compare his diary to mine!

Now, as an indoor rower, you may have this image of me being
quite a big guy. I'm 6ft 2 and 16 and a half stone and many would think
there's no way Wayne, approaching 50 years old can do this. Most people
would look at me and find it difficult to imagine me attempting one stage
of the Tour de France, let alone all of it, but this was all about my dream,
not theirs.

I worked out from Tim's book how to set about the challenge.
I reckoned on covering at least half of the professional's daily riding,
meaning I had to cycle approximately 65 miles a day in less than 6 weeks.
The actual race lasts 3 weeks. My goal became my 'magnificent obsession'
because I was living it every day. I would wake up at 5am thinking about
the Tour de France; there was never any need to remind myself of it! It
was a true vision in my head and everything reminded me of it: looking
at bikes, pictures of the Alps, sunflowers, programmes about France on
the TV. Just seeing the colour purple reminded me of the lavender fields
in Provence: even drinking champagne or sparkling wine would remind
me of my challenge. My vision was all consuming.

I told lots of people about my plans, which can have its
disadvantages. Some people uttered amusement and the people in the

know (other cyclists) uttered disbelief. A colleague, a club cyclist of a good standard on hearing why I was buying a bike he just said, "don't do it mate, it's mad, you're too big and too heavy, you're not a cyclist, you'll kill yourself." Now that's what most people might call well intentioned advice, but I am different. Over the next month I kept getting emails from him saying, "you've got to think about this, I don't think it is a very good idea" – he was determined to talk me round. The amazing thing was that he had totally misunderstood my plan from the beginning. He thought I was going to ride 'Le Tap', which is just one day of the Tour de France in the mountains! When I told him I was doing the whole thing – he just couldn't believe it!

I truly believe now that someone without my resolve wouldn't have lasted and I know I was very stubborn about it all. Whatever was being thrown at me, once I had declared that I was going to do it, I was going to do it! The positive pathways that I had been building in my brain were just so wide that I completely rejected anyone who tried to force me down with their so called 'expert opinion'. How much easier it is to do something when you know exactly what it is you want to do. I recognise now that it was my explicit vision of my inspirational dream that was providing me with the resolve to achieve it.

I also had enormous pride; everyone knew I was a sportsman and everyone knew I had achieved good things, more through hard work as opposed to any natural talent. I was never going to back out. I told my parents and they were so excited about it. My mother said, "Wow that would be great." The people who didn't know about all the barriers and the hardship had no doubts at all.

I was still doing a full time job during my year's preparation. The difficulties of training and trying to secure sponsorship for a motor home, insurances, equipment, fuel, ferries, clothing and more was never ending. I didn't manage to get everything for free; in fact the whole project from start to finish cost me about £3,500. I paid for all the fuel, food and camping sites etc. but happily I secured two ferry crossings from P&O. When a company gave me money it went straight to the charity.

Early on it became clear that I wanted to ride for a charity close to home. Two training staff colleagues at the Lancashire Constabulary Training Centre, Mark Jukes and Keith Butterworth, had both died due to cancer within the previous 12 months. Keith Butterworth ran our basket ball team for some 15 to 20 years, so I was close to him. I therefore decided to ride for the Rosemere Cancer Foundation, which is a local Lancashire cancer charity. This crystallised my desire even further as I wasn't doing it just for me but to raise money for something that was deeply emotional to me. This gave my vision further personal significance.

It would have been bizarre to have spent more money on the event than I could raise for charity. Initially I thought I would spend around £2000 but I went over budget on that. I then got a massive boost from the local Round Table. I sent a letter to Lakeland Willow Water up at Grange over Sands in Cumbria, where the owners had been keen cyclists. Tragically one of them had died of cancer just before the company opened for trading. The surviving founder rang me up and said that although business wasn't good, he would give me as much bottled water that I could carry in any motor vehicle plus a £1000 donation; he was my biggest sponsor. I also received a motor caravan through a friend of a friend at Stuart Longton Caravans. As the year progressed the money grew and grew, so every time I reached a target I increased it by another £1000 and just kept going until eventually my pledges totalled over £10,500.

In addition to fundraising, my training was all consuming and totally inadequate. I had worked out that I would need to do 65-70 miles a day to complete the tour in less than 6 weeks. I reasoned that because I'm twice the age and twice the weight of the expert riders, it would take twice as long. So I had to do all these miles along with my full time job. How was I going to do the mileage and how was I going to prepare for the Alps and the Pyrenees when there isn't anything in this country remotely like it? I asked a cyclist, how do I prepare for the Alps? They said "you can't, it's as simple as that".

The biggest training climbs I did were in the Trough of Bowland in east Lancashire. I would set off on a Sunday from St Annes across the flat Fylde coast, get to the Trough of Bowland, go over a hill; maybe a 10 to 15 minute climb and then cycle back – 60 miles approx. Then I would rest the next day, and then do a 38 mile ride with much bigger hills. I tried to prepare the best that I could, whilst working a full time job, chasing sponsorship, training like a mad man, setting up a website with a tracking device on the motor caravan and more. All these things took a lot of time and effort to sort out and I had never managed anything like that before. I found myself snatching time to get on the turbo trainer during lunchtime at work for an hour; even then everyone laughed at me. One of the cleaners had been on holiday to the Alps and he sponsored me £10 which was brilliant as he didn't earn much money. He brought me his holiday photos of the Alps where he had been walking in the summer and let me borrow them. I stuck them on the wall of the boiler room where the bike was and trained to a Kraftwerk CD. There is one track on the CD called the Tour de France; it is really weird but they keep talking about the Tour de France. I played Kraftwerk Tour de France whilst looking at pictures of the Alps and sweating buckets in the boiler room – this was typical of my Alpine preparation.

My good friend Andy Olgilvie had offered to be my driver and his wife Annie helped out as well. I was having a pint with Andy one night discussing where I was up to and I mentioned that I needed a driver. There was no hesitation. He loves France and wine and his hobby was digital photography.

My visualisation techniques were to imagine the exhilaration of being in the saddle, picturing in my mind's eye long climbs over the monstrous Alps with the snow caps all around; all whilst buckets of perspiration ran onto the boiler room floor. The tarmac would be hot and I imagined the smell of the grass and the fields. I watched some of the Tour de France on the TV when they squirt water on the rider's faces. I imagined myself on a hot road in the middle of France cycling through the irrigation sprays and the exhilaration of how that would feel. The vision was really specific with lots and lots of little details. All through my training, all through the long hours of research, all through the hard work of organising and raising the money, I kept my mind on the vivid pictures and emotions of my goal.

My ultimate dream was of course concerned with finishing the Tour de France route. My mental preparation depended upon me also

describing to myself exactly what it would look like when I finished in
Paris on Saturday the 12th July. It would be the day before the official
2004 Tour de France finished at the same spot. The spectator stands
would be built, a city prepared for the annual finish of, in terms of live
spectators, the biggest sporting event in the world.

I imagined a glorious sunny morning when Andy would park
the van close to the Arc de Triumphe. I cycle up the famous cobbles of
Champs-Elysees and do a lap around the Arc, finishing with both arms
above my head, punching the air, just like many professionals do as they
cross the finish line in the race. We embrace and pop the Champagne.
Inquisitive Parisians take photographs with their mobiles. There are
excessive bouts of grinning all-round. This tiny area of the metropolis
would see the finish of an alternative Tour de France the day before
the real circus came to town. Cosmopolitans suspend their humdrum
schedules to surround us and enthusiastically ask about le Tour de
France Charity Challenge emblazoned all across our shirts. It would feel
brilliant telling everyone the quest was complete.

The compilation of words I employed would be used by my brain
to paint vivid and emotive pictures. My brain knew exactly what success
was going to look like. Triumphant at the Arc!

Although my imaginary videotape was set in the future I pictured
it in my head as actually happening in the present tense. This was a 'real'
present tense illustration of what success would look, feel and be like.
My colourful, accurate, emotionally charged piece of video footage was
played thousands of times in my head during the months of preparation
and weeks of actually cycling le Tour. My mental tape never wore out; in

fact it got more vibrant the more I played it. I was hardwiring my brain, building pathways within and programming it to ensure success.

There were the hard training days when I'd get up in the morning at about 4.30am on a 40 mile bike ride to Southport then jump in the shower, work 4 hours, ride in the boiler room at lunch, shower, sit at my desk with a butty, finish work at about 6pm and cycle 17 miles home to St Annes and then get on the computer and do a bit of planning. I had a lot of support from my family although I think they thought I was mad. I think my stepson Sean was a bit mesmerised by it all.

Then suddenly it was 3 months away, then 2 months and you can never do enough training.

I was retiring a week into 'le Tour' so I used my 'leaving do' as a fundraiser and raised about £400, I even had to organise that, getting 70 to 80 people there and a band and charity auction. It was nice to say farewell to all my buddies. The farewell was tearful. I kissed Julie goodbye; "well that's it then, I'll be home for tea at the end of July". Andy and I got in the van and drove off!

The route took in the full length of France down to the Spanish border, the Pyrenees and then crossed to the south east side of France towards Nice and the coast and then up to the Alps; a couple of days in Switzerland, into Germany and then Paris. That's over 2,250 miles. Luckily a quarter of it wasn't too bad because it was reasonably flat!

After each day's riding my nightly ritual with my large fold out Michelin Map of France was always a treat. I used a highlighter marker and after every day in the saddle I would mark my inch or so progress. After the first week it didn't look too impressive as France is awfully big when compared to England. I was thinking, 'my god, I really am going to spend a long time on this bike'.

It always seemed to be hot and breezy. We started in Midwest France, and went north towards the English Channel without any real problems. Navigation proved to be a massive frustration to me, trying to follow the exact and meandering route. Navigating all over France on your own with a map wrapped in cellophane to keep it dry whilst stuffed down the back of your shorts added to my problems. Rural French sign posts aren't known for their accuracy so they regularly sent me off course.

After 4 or 5 days cycling, I then slipped on the van steps and injured my left knee. This meant for a week I could hardly walk and literally had to lift my leg onto the step to climb into the van.

The funny thing was that I could actually cycle less painfully than I could walk because the pushing action was easier than any lifting action. My injury soon got to the stage where I doubted whether I could carry on. Each day got worse and I was taking more and more painkillers. When I turned south to cycle the full length of France I was pitted against a tortuous head wind for about 7 days at 60 miles a day. I had hoped to build in extra miles in case I fell behind schedule at a later date but that was proving impossible.

We eventually arrived at the foot of the Pyrenees and close to the border with Spain. I set off for my first climb which really was my first big test following a year's preparation. An undulating and sweltering 45 mile ride actually preceded the base of the climb. I paused at the bottom of the climb at a large public information sign for cyclists. I'd already done 3 hours on my bike and it was a roasting hot day, so I read the English version with interest. Basically it was a warning for all cyclists saying 'attempt this at your peril!' I set off and the road became quite narrow. It was probably about 30°C and I was already a little dehydrated from the ride the week before, from which I'd never quite recovered. After every kilometre there is a little stone marker with a bike and a percentage incline for the next kilometre. Very soon the true immensity of my challenge struck home.

I climbed for the early kilometres at an average of 8%, which is quite steep, especially on a bike. Then I hit a 12% section and it tested me to my limit. I started to dread what the next sign would read, praying for single figures. I'd tackled a 15% incline in the Trough of Bowland but only for 5 minutes. That isn't so bad but this was mile after mile of agony, with no respite. You never get a chance to ease off. As the relentless incline got steeper and I got more exhausted and dehydrated (I had run out of drink), things went from bad to worse until I got about two thirds of the way up the hill and I just fell off; I couldn't remain upright for another metre. This was a defining moment.

Even though I had never been in doubt that I could complete the challenge, I still thought 'crikey, this is my first major test, I've failed it miserably'. I was unable to remount my bike because it was so steep. I stood humiliated on the grass verge and had the indignity of awkwardly struggling in my clip shoes for about a kilometre up the hill. That was a serious mental test – it was my first hard ascent and I was walking up it. The true emotional test for me was whether I would crack. I had to show so much resolve at that point there. I had to keep my dream in mind to drive me on.

I took some water and got myself together. Eventually I got to a section where the road widened and the incline lessened a little and I just simply forced myself to carry on. I faced downhill and remounted my bike, got my toe clips in and swiftly did a U turn and started zigzagging uphill again. There were a couple of French paratrooper cyclists who had passed me on the way up waving and whistling, and when I got to the top they gave me a round of applause and congratulated me. The looked like skinned rabbits, strong but sinewy lean. They were riding across the Pyrenees as part of their holiday so I thought they were mad. However, when they gave me water I thought they were wonderful. My descent down the other side was long and scary, but what a relief it was to get over my first major climb, eventually.

There are 5 categories of mountain ascents; this had been a category 1, which is the second hardest. The following day it was going to be a HC ascent which is the most demanding of all in terms of altitude, steepness and length of climb. Translated into English, 'Haute Categorie' means a foreboding 'beyond categorisation'. That night I had some serious conversations with myself.

The next day was a beautiful, almost cloudless day, the kind of perfect day I had been dreaming about. It was a highly demanding 13 mile continuous ascent with stunning scenery to match. I passed Andy in the van on the way up. It was the van's first serious climb of le Tour, and as I creaked passed it, the bonnet was lifted with an overheated engine. The van wasn't the only one overheating I thought. The van cooled and Andy was waiting for me at the summit. It was an unbelievably good climb that could not have gone better. What a contrast to the previous day. There was only one bit of navigation on the ascent and I went wrong and ended up at a ski centre half way up, which indicates how high these mountains were. To put things in perspective – simply think about one of the highest peaks in England, put a road over it then double it in height! Having conquered my first monstrous 'HC' climb, and done it so strongly, I saw no logical reason why I couldn't climb the other six HCs, or indeed the other 35 climbs of lesser difficulty on route. Logic is a wonderful thing when coupled with a strong positive attitude.

The following day there was another HC peak to tackle which we decided I would ride solo. A cold and misty day, with a wet and greasy road meant no one else seemed bothered to make the trip. I simply heaved my bulk skywards through the mist for 2 hours, looked at some clouds and then scared myself witless on the treacherous descent.

The next major moment was when my friend Mark Taylor, a keen cyclist, joined me for 4 days in the South of France. It was good to cycle with someone else; it gave a real boost to my occasionally flagging morale. Two days riding eastwards towards Nice we seemingly always had the infamous Mont. Ventoux in our view and what an amazing and emotion filled experience the ascent turned out to be. Ventoux is the one every cyclist talks about. The famous British cyclist Tom Simpson died less than 2km from the summit during 'le tour' from a combination of drugs, alcohol and supreme effort. It's a straight 11mile hike up to 6,000 ft altitude of exposed volcanic rock. The highest recorded wind speed in Europe was recorded at its barren summit; it's absolutely desolate.

After our morning's cycling we were delayed for 6 hours at the foot of Mont Ventoux because Andy had problems with the van. By 5.30pm the roads had been baking hot all day so there was a lot of heat radiating upwards, and the mistral wind had 'freshened' to put it mildly. We were entering the unknown. Mark and I set off together from its base and our pace soon felt well inside my limitations. We had agreed that if either of us felt good we could just go on ahead at our own pace. After just a couple of miles together I wanted to speed up and climb it in under 2 hours, which is apparently pretty good for a big old bloke like me.

On reflection I physically pushed myself on the climb far too hard and when I passed Simpson's memorial I was in a very fragile physical and emotional state. His memorial is surrounded by memorabilia left by other cyclists. Tom's body had given up on the white pumice lunar landscape through the abuse he had given it. He regularly used amphetamines and brandy for the climbs. No wonder he was so good!

I pushed it, really pushed it, and was climbing so strongly I felt like I was dancing on the pedals. After passing Tom's memorial I made it to the 6,000 ft summit, but the thinner air and my over zealous efforts magnified my emotions. For a brief time I 'cracked' at the top and my resulting summit video diary was akin to a Certificate 18 film! Not a pretty sight.

Mark returned home all too soon as I headed northwards from Nice. My biggest test lay ahead of me, along the entire backbone of the French Alps and into Switzerland. I was getting very impatient all the way through the Alps and Andy was trying to get me to take a day off and rest, but I just wanted to get to Paris. It was pleasurable in a perverse way, but I just wanted to get it done and go home.

I'd lost about a stone and a half prior to the tour and lost half a stone during the tour so I was pretty lean by the end of it and easily going through 20 to 30 pints of water per day. I couldn't eat enough calories: most of my fuel came from a huge bowl of porridge in the morning 2 hours before cycling and power drinks all day, with carbohydrate and protein drinks and a meal at night. But I would wake up in the night just having to drink water it was so hot in the van. Towards Switzerland and then Germany it really heated up. I'd set off from the bottom of an Alp and it would be 25°C. I would get to the top in a hailstorm at 9,000 ft after doing a continuous 26km climb. It was mind boggling.

All this time, the thing that kept me going was my dream; the vision. A big part of that was seeing Julie again and that led to another big moment for me. Whilst cycling towards a horrendously tough summit I saw a woman walking down towards me. From a distance, just for a couple of seconds, it looked like Julie had flown out to encourage me, but it wasn't. I 'lost it' big time.

By the time we reached Germany I was getting so impatient to finish. We had a V-Sol vehicle satellite tracking device fitted and my own website recorded our location so that supporters and sponsors could track me round France. They could see that suddenly I was cranking up some big mileage and when they expected the van to stop, it didn't. On the final day heading on to Paris, I did the highest mileage of my tour which was a full Stage covering 127 miles; I had decided to end with a flourish and reckon I did so in style.

After 5 weeks and 3 days of enormous physical efforts, aches and pains, mental trials, disagreements with Andy, horrendous map reading problems, loneliness and, especially, a disintegrating bum, arriving in

Paris was absolutely fantastic. Yet for me it was hard to be outwardly ecstatic even when we cracked open the champagne. I simply felt comfortable with myself. I had always had this vision that it was going to be massively celebratory and ecstatic; pumping my fist and doing all that, especially as I had just cycled all the way around the traffic chaos of the Arc de Triumphe (navigation of which, especially by bike, cannot fail to get the adrenaline pumping!). Andy handed me a bottle of champagne, we supped it, and I just started crying. Everything about the moment was all such a relief. Utter relief. I phoned Julie and simply said "I've only gone and done it haven't I? I've cycled the Tour de France!"

We raised over £10,700 for the Rosemere Cancer Foundation. I achieved something that very few people can ever say they have done. My ambitious goal helped me recruit the amazing support of so many people, and without their help it would not have been possible. Thank you all.

I completed the Tour de France properly, no skirting around mountains and no short cuts. I did it when lots of people believed it was impossible. I have done something worthy and unbelievably challenging, and now I can always look back and say; 'yes, I really did do that!'

Wayne's story shows that even when others doubt you; even when they doubt your sanity; a well formed DayDream will keep you motivated to the end. Against all the odds Wayne achieved his ultimate dream and more. Visualising it correctly drove him not only in committing to it, but also in the preparation and even during the ride itself.

What did you take on board from Wayne's incredible journey? Record your thoughts below.

RuleThree
**TheDevil
IsInTheDetail**

3

Make your inspirational dream specific.

Many people have heard of SMART goals[1]. The S stands for specific. Think of your dream as a laser beam rather than a floodlight. Remember that a picture paints a thousand words. You may not want to stretch to a thousand words to describe your picture, but the more detail you have in there, the more likely that this picture is personal to you.

Adding the detail makes the picture clearer. It gives you a more accurate destination for the journey towards your goal. Think about Satellite Navigation in a car. If you programme it to take you to London, it will find its version of the centre. If you punch in Upper Street in Islington, and maybe even include the postcode too, it will find that very location, specific to your requirements. How you set goals works in the same way. Aim for what you REALLY want, not just a vague idea of it.

As you picture your goal, take time to look around and view the scene. Add some details around you. What may at first seem insignificant, even a little indulgent, will add clarity and depth to your DayDream.

Try to include as many senses as possible in your picture. Ask yourself; "what can I…

- **See**
- **Hear**
- **Feel** (physically and mentally)
- **Taste**
- **Smell"**

Some senses are more powerful in certain situations than others. Remember to go beyond simply seeing it happen. Often, the other, less obvious senses add much needed clarity and richness to your picture.

Example: **Living Space**

A delegate I met on a course recently achieved a goal that was important to him. He underwent a successful extension of his house, including a larger kitchen, dining area and conversion of outhouses into a downstairs toilet and utility/laundry room. The achievement of this goal, he knew, would take much time, money, inconvenience and effort. He told me that focusing on his inspirational dream drove him to keep digging deeper (into his pockets as well as the ground I presume!).

He wrote this DayDream in January 2006:

It is June 2006 and I am stood at the end of our new breakfast bar. All our friends are collected in the new kitchen and the buzz is tremendous. Loud music bounces from the wall mounted speakers and the smell of the barbeque wafts in through the new French doors. The salads sit proudly on the table and the bottles bang loudly in the new bin as someone finishes another beer. My gin and tonic feels cold in my hand as I sip gently, catching the zesty smell and enjoying the cool

*sensation on this warm summer's evening. Standing there,
looking at my friends' and family's smiling faces, the humdrum
of chatter reaching a crescendo, I know we have finally done it!
We can be proud of all our choices. It looks as good as
the brochures!*

The detail is so fantastic in his story that it paints a picture
in *my* mind, and it's not even my goal. As with many building
projects, he didn't *quite* finish on time! However, missing his
deadline by a couple of weeks was an insignificant issue when
that party finally took place.

My colleague Richard insists on including smells in his
DayDreams. The funny thing is, when he describes the smell
of grass in his vision of canoeing the Caledonian Canal across
Scotland, I swear everyone closes their eyes, raises their nose to
the air and smells the grass themselves!

With any DayDream, when you really start to create a
detailed picture, there is always the debate as to whether it
should happen *exactly* as you have visualised. To my mind this
does not matter. As long as you still achieve the goal that the
DayDream applies to, then surely this is the important result.
Often, as your behaviour drives you towards, and ultimately to
accomplish, your goal, the picture will be lived out in much of its

detail, as it is this specificity that has driven you. If it doesn't, you have two choices.

- **You can be happy with the fact that you have achieved your goal you set out to achieve and not worry too much about the picture living itself out**
- **You can set out to 'recreate' the picture to give you the final sense of achievement if you need to**

Either way, you have still achieved your goal.

Take the following example from a great book by James Cracknell and Ben Fogle called 'The Crossing'. It charts the story of their momentous journey across the Atlantic in one of the world's toughest rowing races. James Cracknell writes; *"Ever since setting off I'd visualised our arrival in Antigua: rowing into a lagoon full of bright turquoise water, grounding the boat on the golden sand, jumping out of the boat into warm, knee high water and running up the beach into the arms of Bev and Croyde."* Interestingly, Cracknell knew that they would actually come into a harbour full of boats and that this 'perfect vision' would not take place exactly as he saw it. This didn't matter to him. His DayDream still drove him beyond the limits of endurance.

You need to be careful with specificity however.

Throughout the book, Fogle describes his dream of simply finishing, reaching Antigua; Cracknell, with his enormously competitive streak that has led him to take Olympic Gold in rowing, talks only of winning. Interestingly, with only a short distance to go, a support boat tells them that they 'have it in the bag'. They are way ahead and can afford to enjoy crossing the line first. It is at that point (after weeks of sheer hell) that Cracknell's body finally gives way. In his mind they have won already. His DayDream is achieved. It was Fogle, whose DayDream was primarily in the finishing, that rowed most of the way in those final moments. He brought them in.

You can lose weight for a wedding day, but what about after? You can work hard for an all important exam, but what about the other things you need to work hard for? Think carefully about this as you build your picture.

We are actually all very good at forming detailed pictures.

Take a long look around you now. Think about the things that surround you. Notice some of the details. Now close your eyes and describe the scene as you saw it. I will wager that if you take enough time, you can recount much of the detail in that picture. All you are doing here is recalling a picture from your past. Whether this is recent or distant past actually shouldn't matter too much.

My example of this comes from my wedding day. This was an event that I feel particularly happy about and pretty proud of actually. It is one of my most treasured memories and an event in my life that gives me huge amounts of pleasure.

When I think about the day itself, it evokes many feelings, including those of love, pride, joy, excitement, anticipation and much more.

My picture of the day, however, is not perhaps what I, nor others, would have expected. It was 1.30 and I can see myself sat in the corner of the pub. We were to be married in the pub at 3pm that afternoon. People were arriving and already the bar area was getting full. I was sat in a big wooden chair with the open fire roaring at the far side of the room. On one side of me sat my wonderful cousin Chris and on the other, the brilliant Ben and Ginny. The music was loud enough to be heard over the hum of voices. My Dad walked into the room and asked everyone what they would like to drink. I suddenly had to think about what my LAST drink would be as a single man!! Guinness was the only answer I could think of that would do it justice. I am sat in my suit, staring at a beautiful pint of the black stuff, plush in my new suit, excited, ready to go. Ready to go.

If we are so good at using this ability to construct pictures then there is no reason why we cannot do exactly the same for something that will happen in the future as for something that has happened in the past.

[1]SMART – A commonly used method of setting goals, whereby the goals are – Specific, Measurable, Achievable, Realistic & Timed.

TopTips

- Add your personality to the DayDream; this will give you detail. Give it your own personal touches
- Include all 5 senses if you can
- Close your eyes and picture the DayDream as you would with a memory. Take time to enjoy it and your mind will fill the detail in

This is a great way to look at how we can find inspiration in order to form our pictures properly. We do it all the time when we use our memories.

In the first column opposite, list five events from your life that make you happy or that you feel particularly proud of.

Now with those five events, write down what feelings you associate with them in the second column. Think about this hard and try to get past the first couple of words in each case. It may be that you use a number of the same words in the different examples. This is fine.

Now re-create the 'Polaroid picture' of that event in your mind's eye. Think hard about what happened. Which is the first picture that springs to mind? Which is the strongest picture that springs to mind? Describe it to yourself. Write down the details. I have written my wedding day Polaroid in as an example.

As you work through your examples, try to see, hear, feel, taste and smell everything around you in that Polaroid picture. Think about it in all its detail. When you think you have seen enough, take one extra look around your mind's eye and then pick out another detail of this condensation of your memory log.

EVENT	FEELINGS	POLAROID
My Wedding Day	Love, Pride, Anticipation, Excitement, Happiness, Joy	Guinness in the corner

I am sure you will be able to pick out far more than you may have originally thought possible.

As you have thought about this you have actually undergone a very similar process to thinking about and visualising your DayDreams. It's just that you have done this for something that has already happened rather than using your imagination to construct a picture for something yet to happen.

As you apply all the lessons from this book to the construction of your DayDreams, remember the amount of detail you recall from these pictures of the past and make sure that you emulate this for future goals.

Exercise: **Polaroid pictures**

"You have to have a
dream so you can get
up in the morning."

BILLY WILDER

RuleFour
GiveYourself
GooseBumps

4

Make it emotive (and perhaps even emotional!)
Remember the equation:

$$\text{Intensity} \times \text{Frequency} = \text{Bandwidth}$$
$$I \times F = B$$

Whereas the purest form of the goal may seem a little dry, uninspiring and perhaps even boring when written out in the traditionally understood way, the DayDream should make the hairs stand up on the back of your neck.

It is no secret that people are usually much better at achieving a goal when they have a well formed inspirational dream. One only has to look at how much better people are at losing weight for a particular event such as a wedding day or a holiday!

The reason why this is so effective is because people tap into their deepest reserves of drive and energy to achieve a goal through the generation of DESIRE. The physical reason for this is that the more intense or emotive a thought process is, the greater the volume of chemicals that pass along the pathway in your brain. The greater the volume of chemicals, the more bandwidth that thought creates in terms of those pathways. You build your mental muscle more quickly. Remember, the wider you build a pathway, the easier and indeed the more likely it is that your behaviour will follow that pathway – the quicker it becomes your behavioural 'path of least resistance'.

When you really WANT something, it is far more likely that you will do everything it takes to get there. That desire is created by the emotional attachment you give to something. The emotional attachment is created by the dream behind your goal. Therefore, take advantage of this simple link between your emotions and your ability to achieve things. The more emotive this is, the more effective it is in driving you towards the destination.

Think about Wayne's story. He created desire by his emotional connection with cancer. He had lost people to cancer and so riding for that cause naturally increased his passion to succeed.

When writing your DayDream, think about your personal 'hooks'. What is it about this goal that really lights YOUR candle? Nobody loses weight because they want to lose weight. People lose weight to look great for a party, to feel good on the beach, to fit into a dress, to run a marathon and more. Ask yourself 'What is your hook?' WHY do you want to do this?

Example: **Losing Weight**

A good friend of mine, by his own admission, loves his food a little too much! This is far from a major problem but he was overweight enough to know that it could well affect his health in the future. More importantly to him in the short term though, was that he felt embarrassed when in any state of semi-nakedness (changing rooms and beach wear come to mind).

The goal therefore was to 'lose some weight'.

The DayDream read as follows and was written in 2004.

It is August 2005 and I am walking down the most beautiful palm fringed beach in The Maldives, holding hands with my wife as we chat in the early evening sunset. We amble slowly along in the warm shallow water enjoying the cool breeze. In a moment we will head back to the house to get ready for another stunning beachside meal. But for now, there is just time for one last swim. I turn and jump into the waves topless, fit and proud! Splash!

I could name any number of friends and family who have managed to shed those extra pounds and feel at their best just in time for an important event. Why? Because if looking slim on that day is important enough to them (which it often is) the emotiveness of that vision outweighs the emotiveness of eating the next chocolate bar. The bandwidth you build for looking and feeling great on that day is wider than the bandwidth for the 'extra biscuit or three'.

It is incredible how effective we are at achieving goals when we set them properly, inspirationally and in a way that uses our brain correctly.

When we set goals effectively, when we create the DayDream that taps into our desire, when we give a more powerful instruction to our brain to work for us as opposed to against us, the sky is the limit.

As you can see, these rules are simply formalising what we already do. Perhaps we have never realised it until now, but as humans, we are already experts at DayDreaming.

TopTips

- **Make the hairs stand up on the back of your neck**
- **Think of your personal hooks**
- **Determine the underlying reason for your goal**

"Imagination is everything. It is the preview of life's coming attractions."

ALBERT EINSTEIN

Football in the blood

Mike Mair

Football was a part of my life as far back as I can actually remember; playing out in the street, very young, as a schoolboy no more than 5 years old. My mum and dad cut articles and reports out of the paper and put them into a scrap book and all that sort of stuff.

It was central to my life, because it was central to my dad's life. He was involved in a junior football club called Mugiemoss and then Dyce Juniors. The term 'juniors' in this context doesn't refer to the age group; it's a standard of football. Junior football players are paid to play now and, even though in those days they weren't, it was still a fairly high standard of football. Some players even went on to be professionals. The junior football club Mugiemoss amalgamated with another club in the early 80s to form Dyce Juniors and their ground was renamed Ian Mair Park in honour of my dad after he died. He had been involved for 35 years.

You could also say that I was a hugely dedicated supporter of Aberdeen FC, not just through my geographical roots, but also this link through my father and the feeder system.

My main memory of Aberdeen as a youngster was that Dad never took me to games on a Saturday because he was always involved with his own club. When Aberdeen won the Scottish cup in 1970, my dad had gone to that game and the next day he came back and he took me to see them coming home with the cup. There were over 100,000 people in the city centre. I can remember watching that and afterwards being desperate to go to a game. The first games he ever took me to were a Scotland international and then an Aberdeen European night. At school in 1971, we had been offered tickets for Scotland versus Belgium at Pittodrie, which was on a Wednesday night and the following week Aberdeen were playing Juventus in the UEFA cup.

He took me to both games, under the floodlights, capacity crowds both times, 30,000 plus, and it was just magical. I can still see visions of it now. It was amazing and Joe Harper was my hero.

He went away to Everton, came back to Hibernian and then Aberdeen brought him back again. He was a legend.

As a supporter, I was very lucky to support Aberdeen when they last started to win things in Scotland. I was only 20 years old when they won the Cup Winner's Cup. To witness that and to be able to be part of it was prime time.

As a school boy, my dream was to play for club and country. I was a good amateur player but at that time there were a lot of good players running around in Aberdeen. Three guys I used to play against eventually played for Aberdeen in a European Cup Winner's Cup final team! After the guys got the opportunity to go professional, I was playing in a youth team and was actually picked to play for Aberdeen under 18s youth select. That side was selected after the best players had moved on. Therefore, it was probably about the time I was 16 that I realised my dream was never going to happen.

Since then I have had years of supporting Aberdeen, years of following Scottish football, travelling around the world. I have been to World Cups and European Championships. I've been to Italy, Belgium, Holland, Germany and France. I never thought I would have had the chance to put on the shirts and play for the teams I loved so much.

I came on a course run by Simon and wrote down my goals and a very odd thing happened. It was so odd that it was almost coincidental. One of my mates, Rich, introduced the idea of 'football aid'. I had never heard about football aid, so he explained what it was about. I saw it on the website and the next day was on the phone asking "is this for real? I'll get us booked in". Football Aid is a charity where, in exchange for raising money, people 'play' for their club in a game staged at the stadium. You use the full dressing rooms, the players' lounge and wear the kits provided. The only difference is that the stadium isn't quite so full! This became my goal. To play for Scotland at Hampden Park! It had always been my goal, but I presumed that I was past the chance of course.

From the time I knew I was going to get the chance to play, which was probably 9 months before the big day itself, every day I was picturing making a tackle, winning a header, passing the ball; every day I was thinking about playing. I imagined walking out on the pitch, listening to the anthems, having some friends around me playing and waving at Sonia and Lewis (my wife and son) in the crowd with other friends, wives and children. I pictured the game in full flow with great tackles, good passes and a shot at goal, certainly a header at goal. It was mostly about defending strong and true. I could feel the badge on my heart. I was even visualising arriving the night before, staying in the hotel, the pre match meal, getting ready in the plush changing rooms, everything. This was a 9 month vision to play well.

Winning is everything to me. The guys that played in the other team would have enjoyed the experience but there was no way they would enjoy it as much as we were going to. We were going to win.

My behaviour followed straight away. Number 1: to get fit. There was no way I was going to be there and be like a carthorse. I couldn't imagine anything worse than not playing well.

Before we got the go ahead I went to the gym probably twice a week; it was really just keeping healthy as opposed to keeping fit. I was starting to increase how much I was doing on a weekly basis and, 6 months before the date, I would be training almost every day.

It would mean every day doing something after Lewis had gone to bed. I would go to the gym or for a long walk with weights strapped to my back. On summer nights I'd go for a cycle; I could cycle quite a good way because it didn't put any pressure on the joints.

I also had to raise the money, as it was all for charity. To play in the Scotland game we had to raise £700 as a minimum. Even if I hadn't have raised any of the money I would have found it somehow.

I did all this despite having a dodgy knee. I had it in my mind that by training I could compensate. After moving to Cambridge many years ago, I did play football at a reasonable level and then I had a bad injury. They told me that if I wanted to play at a similar standard again, I would need a serious operation. I've actually had 5 operations due to football injuries.

There were four lifelong friends that I grew up with from Aberdeen; Arthur, my best man at my wedding; Dave, who was an usher; Rich, who gave a reading and Lindsay, who was also in the wedding party. I'd been friends with them since we were school boys and they were going to play at Hampden Park with me! Also, Paul, a colleague from my playing days in Cambridge would be there. It was pretty emotional in the changing room before we went out. I think it was quite clear in the

*conversations before we went out that we were not going to let anyone
down; we were really nervous and hyped up.*

*On the day we were up in the lounge looking over the stadium,
which is awesome, and they asked the players to come walking down
which was when you actually realise, hey, this is it!*

*We walked down into the tunnel; there was a piper playing outside
and they were playing a tape that sounded like there were 50,000 people
outside in the stadium.*

*I walked down with a lump in my throat and a tear in my eye.
I could hear all the families shouting, I could actually hear Lewis and
Sonia, so I turned round and waved to them. We got into position for
the National Anthem, at which point I started thinking about my dad.
Very quickly the National Anthem played and suddenly I was saying to
myself, 'this is it' and then the focus was totally on playing well. In some
of the photographs taken before the game, I was trying to smile, but you
are just so focussed on enjoying this game. I walked along, shaking hands
and a guy comes along with a number 9 on and he does look a bit older. I
thought I was going to be OK but it turns out it was number 11 playing
against me! He looked the part; turns out this guy that I was up against
was an ex-Hearts (a Scottish Premiership team) youngster!*

*This guy was still playing for non-league football in Scotland, but
that probably worked better that I was actually up against somebody
who knew what he was doing. I like to think as a defender I handled him
pretty well.*

*My first touch was all important; the ball was played to me and I
passed it wide to Lindsay. That's when I really felt like I was on my way.*

We won 5 nil. I felt really in control, keeping my shape and putting all the essential tackles in.

We were so determined right to the last. They got a penalty, we were under a bit of pressure during the game, but I thought that we defended really well. All my mates were of the same attitude so that made a big difference. Before the penalty, I remember going up to Paul saying 'save this, save this', and he did!

I lived my dream. It was just a perfect day, but it didn't stop there. I had an appetite for this dream!

After the game they came over and asked if we would do it again next year. I agreed to consider it if the game would be at Aberdeen. Aberdeen hadn't taken part for two or three years.

The guy came back to us and told us they weren't interested. I made sure he knew this was a big disappointment and he asked me to send an email. A couple of weeks later they came back to me; 'you'll never guess what; Aberdeen has agreed to do it now!'

I don't know whether I made the club reconsider, but perhaps it was a part. I have no doubt my dream was pushing me to keep going all the way. I had played for my country at the national stadium and I then went on to represent Aberdeen at Pittodrie.

It's fair to say as soon as getting the go ahead from Aberdeen, getting in contact with all my mates; we were desperate to play again. We went through the same all over again in terms of the vision of playing at Aberdeen and what would happen on the day itself. This time I had some experience to draw upon for my dream! I trained and trained for my home town debut.

I missed a lot of the things in the first game so the second time round I made a conscious effort to take more of it in. I felt more confident after the experience of what happened at Hampden, surrounded by more of my friends; three of us actually played in the same school championship-winning team in 1974. I knew that the desire was 100% to win this game. The result was never in doubt; 6-1. In the photograph pre-match I was smiling more this time, but nevertheless, we were well revved up. Our manager for that game was John Hewitt who scored the winning goal in the European Cup Winner's Cup Final against Real Madrid and I used to play against him at schoolboy level. We reminisced about our schoolboy days when we used to kick lumps out of each other and talked about how our lives had gone different ways. He was chuffed to bits that I was fulfilling my dream playing for Aberdeen. I suppose to give him his credit though; he did it the proper way!

I thought about my Dad a lot. He would have been very emotional I'm sure. He gave me huge support with regards to football, even whilst knowing that I would probably never be a professional. My mother and my sister were actually at the Aberdeen game, and they had never been to Aberdeen's stadium before.

I believe that any young boy, who loves football, has a dream to play for club and country and there are only a few that actually achieve it.

I've done it in a creative way but it meant just as much. In fact, even doing it in that creative way, it still meant so much to me that I probably felt the same as if I had done the real thing!

Mike's story shows that if a DayDream is important enough; if it is emotive enough, then you will find a way to achieve it. It may not be the expected, traditional or usual way, but you will find a way! Where there is enough will, there will be a way! Some goals may be too lofty – but with some creativity, you can still live your dream of sorts. As Mike says; it doesn't matter, it is just as much an achievement and he feels just as good about it now.

Was it luck that an opportunity presented itself to Mike soon after he had written his goals and pictured his vision? It was no coincidence. Mike's filter put two and two together. If it wasn't that, I am sure that he would have found another way; consciously or not.

What did you learn from Mike's story? Note down your thoughts below.

Notes

RuleFive
Don'tLook
NowBut

...

5

Use Positive Pictures Only

Don't think of a pink Elephant…

It's impossible isn't it? Your brain cannot picture things in the negative so your DayDream needs to be written in the positive. This is especially relevant to a goal that involves giving up a bad habit, overcoming a phobia or where you would have to STOP doing something. However, it applies to all goals. You need to imagine what you WANT out of something. This also helps you to generate the emotion in your DayDream.

Just try it with a friend in the pub. 'Don't look now but…' is the surest way to turn their head straight away! Have you ever tried to tell a child NOT to step in the puddle? What does that child then do? Splash!

The words have painted a picture in the child's brain. A physical connection has formed because the child has imagined doing exactly what you told them not to. Combine this with the emotion that a child associates with splashing in a puddle, FUN, and suddenly you have created a picture for the child, which their brain cannot help but drive towards achieving!

The same principles work when you think of things that you don't want. Your brain doesn't know whether this is good or bad for you. You build pathways with every thought you ever have. If you try to imagine not doing something, it will inevitably lead to you imagining the very thing you don't want to do. If this is the case, then you build a pathway which will drive behaviours towards that thing.

Example: **To Smoke or not to smoke?**

The goal is to give up smoking.

It is Christmas Day 2008 and I am sat in the front room, sipping a cool beer whilst Christmas classics blast out from the stereo. The fire is roaring and warming the air, casting a soothing glow over everyone's faces. Everyone's presents are opened and wrapping paper is strewn over the floor. We will tidy up in a minute. I haven't had a cigarette in nearly 6 months and now that I no longer smoke I feel fantastically healthy.

Now, at first sight, this looks like a great DayDream, which has taken into account all our rules so far. The issue here is that negative language has been used. As soon as I mentioned smoking and cigarettes it makes me think of the very thing I am trying to give up.

A delegate on a course once told a colleague of mine about a DayDream he had written in order to help him in his fight to give up smoking.

It is Christmas Eve and my wife and I are walking down the main street in our local village. We are on our way to our favourite restaurant, a ritual we repeat every year. The kids are tucked up in bed, excited about their presents. To be honest, we are more excited than they are! I can hear my shoes, crunching against fresh snow and I can see my breath condense into the crisp night sky. Everything shimmers white. We turn into the door of the restaurant and throw it open. The music, the voices, the heat and the smell of garlic hit us like a ton of bricks as we walk into the bar. The waiter takes our coats and sits us at a table by the open fire. He brings over our favourite bottle of Italian Red and pops the cork. Later our main courses arrive, I have ordered fillet steak with Diane sauce and my knife runs through the meat like butter. I take a piece along with a swig of the wine and breathe up into my nose as I chew. It tastes absolutely fantastic. I swallow and breathe out and can feel my shoulders relax. Aaaaaaah!

A colleague of his asked how this vision, this DayDream shows that he has given up smoking by Christmas Eve. His reply was short and sweet. *"If you had smoked as long and hard as I had, then you wouldn't be able to taste your food and wine properly either."*

He managed to find his hook, using positive language only. To him, giving up smoking meant that he would be able to enjoy his meals again. For others it may be about playing football again, or even just getting up the stairs. He called us in October. He had woken up one morning and just 'stopped'. He 'just didn't fancy one'. He demanded his office be redecorated as he couldn't face the smell! He said it was then he knew he was a truly 'reformed smoker'. In the past he had only ever forced his behaviour, without actually having a picture in his mind of the end result he wanted. All he had ever told himself was that he wanted to 'stop smoking'. Try thinking about 'not smoking' a cigarette without visualising the very thing you want to give up.

Painting YOUR picture means exactly that. The DayDream is yours and yours alone. If it is something you want to stop doing or avoid, find your hook, whatever it means to you; you can write into your DayDream.

Mike didn't picture himself 'not getting injured or 'not losing the game' did he? Why – because that would be ridiculous. How many times do you play not to lose as opposed to playing to win? How many times do you hear of a sports team becoming nervous and 'protecting against a loss', which results in them tightening up and doing the very thing they were trying to 'protect against'? You must picture what you want.

Example: **Biting Nails**

A friend of mine wrote a DayDream in order to give up the habit of biting his nails. This may sound insignificant but to him it was hugely important. He had been biting his nails for as long as he could remember. So much so that it had become both painful and embarrassing; painful because he bit them so far down and embarrassing because he was now a grown adult struggling to eradicate a perceived childish habit. He had tried everything. He had even become addicted to the bad tasting nail polish his mother had forced him to paint his nails with!

The goal therefore was to 'stop biting his nails'.

The inspirational dream read as follows although I am not sure of the date.

It is (future date) and I am presenting to the board of a large plc on how we will help their people buy into the coming changes in process. As I stand I put my left hand up to the flip chart. I notice the light glint off my gold watch and my wedding ring. I register in that instant that I have "white bits" at the ends of my nails. My nails look great and my hands feel clean and fresh. I walk over to the desk where the HR Director is sitting. I offer my hand out to shake hands on a deal that will ensure our partnership over the coming months. A huge smile creeps over my face as I almost show off my white bits!

Rather than 'forcing himself to not bite his nails' he began to picture the end result as he wanted it. He tells me they aren't perfect, and every now and then he has a nibble or two; but they are far better than they ever were and he does indeed have 'white bits'!

Use only positive language. In doing so, paint the picture of what you want out of the goal.

TopTips

- **Avoid the use of negative words where possible – eg. Not, Don't, Haven't etc.**
- **Find the reason WHY and describe this picture**
- **Use those positive hooks, rather than describing the very thing you want to avoid**

Every goal has a positive hook; every goal has a reason why it is important. It may not be the actual goal itself, but if you have a hook, just like a fish, you will be caught by it. The hook gives you the motivation; that hook is the true reason. Let me give you an example:

As I lie on this bed in a hotel far from home writing this book, my goal is arrive home tomorrow at a reasonable hour. The hook or the reason is to kiss my wife, enjoy dinner together, talk about our day and 'fall into the couch' after a busy day and tiring journey home. It's a simple hook, but just because something is simple does not mean it isn't powerful.

Think of five goals and list them below.

Exercise: **Hooks**

138

Think of the main reasons WHY you want to achieve these goals. Try to find at least one reason for each. These are your HOOKS.

Exercise: **Hooks**

Make sure you build hooks into your DayDreams. This will ensure that you use positive language.

"If you want to reach a goal, you must see the reaching in your own mind before you actually arrive at it."

ZIG ZIGLAR

Rule Six
Nothing Compares To You

6

No comparisons.

Avoid, if you can, making 'competitive' comparisons to other people or things. By competitive, I mean those comparisons that directly pitch you against others. There are a number of reasons for this but two are especially important.

Firstly, you have no idea and, for that matter, usually no control over another individual's behaviour and therefore level of performance.

Let's say that your goal is to improve at golf. Your dream may be to hold a trophy at the annual prize giving at your local golf club; your victory being the highlight of a year of improvement in your game. The speech you make and your name chiselled into one of the mahogany plaques adorning the walls may add detail to the picture. However, the big issue here is that to win, you have to play 'better' than anyone else that day. The truth is you have no control over how anyone else will play. This is difficult terrain and it must be tread carefully.

Secondly, you could actually achieve your goal by sitting still; by default.

To become 'richer', in monetary terms, than Richard Branson could be achieved just as easily by Branson's downfall as by your own rise. If Branson goes bankrupt tomorrow, as long as you are solvent, you have achieved your goal without really hitting the heights you may have intended. My colleague rides mountain bikes competitively. He avoids comparing himself to friends directly, citing the occasion when his friend's chain snapped in the early stages of a race. "I had already beaten him by riding just one extra metre," says Richard. "If beating him had been my goal, then where is the motivation after that?"

There may be a couple of circumstances where you could include a comparison.

1. Performance goals and outcome goals

Many experts talk about the importance of performance goals as well as outcome goals.

- **Performance goals are those that focus on achieving an absolute measurable target. For example: a particular time for a marathon or a monetary sales target.**
- **Outcome goals are those that focus on a result that may involve a relative comparison. For example: to finish first in a marathon or to win the sales person of the year award – beating others to the crown.**

I firmly believe the two can and should be combined. You can be very specific about your absolute performance level in order to help you achieve the relative outcome you desire. Clive Woodward talked time and time again of his desire to make England the number 1 rugby team in the world. This was the relative outcome goal, because it automatically compares the team against others in the world. He also insisted that everyone had absolute performance related goals to help with that.

As long as you include this 'absolute performance' as well as the 'relative outcome', you give your brain, and therefore your behaviour, something solid to aim for. Taking our golfing example a step further – winning the thing may be very important to you. Therefore, including this relative outcome in the inspirational dream may be unavoidable. However, I would encourage you to include the absolute score with which you won it. It is here that you must use your judgement as to what score will win. After you achieve that score, should it not be good enough to win, you need to be prepared to look positively at the fact that you did everything you could and that other events were out of your control.

2. Passive comparisons

There can also be much power in the use of 'passive' comparisons, where you use others as a point of reference rather than as a direct comparison.

Example: **I want to be like Tiger**

My nephew Joe wants to be just like Tiger Woods. He wants to lower his golf handicap significantly. His DayDream could be as follows:

I roll the final putt into the hole on the 18th green, knowing my score in the seventies will mean a cut in my handicap. The shadows are long in the evening sun. It is the end of summer and the birds whistle in the trees. As the ball hits the back of the hole and drops in, I punch the air like Tiger Woods, and shake hands with my opponent.

Here I have used Tiger Woods as a reference point, an image, rather than a performance marker. The question then is: where do you set the target?

On the subject of golf, here is a great example of a DayDream written and carried out by a delegate on a course I ran some time ago.

It is October 17th 2007, I am in Spain having finished the last round of our golf trip. We are on the terrace with the sun shining over the rolling hills of the course, with a nice cold pint of lager in my hand. I step forward to receive the 'Nearest the Pin' trophy with my friends clapping in congratulation – me feeling happy that I had 5 days of fun and knowing I had finished 4th out of 8, a great trip."

Tony scored well for the first two days then he had a bad day where he claims he 'returned to normality'. He then went on to record his highest ever points total on the final day – an 'absolute score' that enabled him to beat everyone on the day and finish, you guessed it, 4th for the week. The resulting outcome was exactly as he described it in the DayDream. The pint of beer was nice and cold; he won 'Nearest the Pin' trophy; he finished 4th (out of 8) and won best individual round trophy.

A large factor where you set your performance level or outcome will be what you BELIEVE to be possible. Rule number 7 will focus on this area.

TopTips

- **Give yourself absolute targets as appropriate. Judge yourself by hitting those targets**
- **Once you have hit that target and achieved the DayDream, you can then stretch your targets for next time.**
- **Combine performance absolutes with the desired outcome**
- **Reference yourself with others but only compete against yourself**

"A goal properly set is a goal halfway reached."

PRESIDENT ABRAHAM LINCOLN

"Don't die with the music in you" –
Wayne Bennett

Nick
Shakibai

Well, it's hard to know where to start really. My friend Simon asked me to write a few words for him on account of the fact that he was putting a book together. It was to be a collection of individual stories based on individual experiences and he wanted me to write one. Me, I felt flattered, then scared, really scared. When it comes to talking, I have no problems getting the hind legs off a donkey, but writing ... well, that's a different story. Still, here we are. So, as a wise man once said: start at the beginning.

I was born on the 21st December 1972 at Stepping Hill Hospital in Stockport. My mother was a recently qualified doctor and my father worked for a photographic processing laboratory in Manchester. We lived in a pleasant semi-detached house in Cheadle for my first 2 years before moving to a large detached house in Wilmslow where I would remain until I left home to go to university 17 years later. The point that I'm trying to make is that I came from a good middle class family and wanted for nothing. I'm not telling you this for effect. No, I'm trying to give you some kind of an idea about what it was like being me.

I attended Ladybarn House School in Cheadle until the age of 7 and then The Kings School in Macclesfield until the age of 16. During my youth, my parents became ever successful. My mother progressed to be a highly respected GP working at 2 practices in the local area. My father had set up his own printing and processing laboratory when I was 3 and now owned one of the largest labs in the north of England. He had followed his dream into the world of photography and better still, was very good at it! His dream just happened to make him a nice bit of cash too. Naturally, with both parents baring such heavy workloads, my sister and I were predominantly looked after by a series of nannies and au-pairs. What little free time my father did have, he chose to spend on the golf course, often playing 36 holes on a Saturday and a further 36 holes on a Sunday. My mother shortly followed, albeit because she quickly realised that she would never see my father again if she didn't!

Now I need to make it clear that this style of upbringing is not something that I hold a bitter resentment for. My parents loved me, of that there is no doubt. They were always taught, through their own, independent upbringing, that the correct way to nurture children was to work and provide for them so they would want for nothing. This meant concentrating on work and earning as much money as possible to be able to provide the best for Stephanie, my sister, and I. Education, holidays, clothes and food … whatever was needed was provided.

The point of all this history is that what went on around me formed the basis for my thoughts and beliefs as I got older. This in turn formed the basis for my goal setting and standards for achievement. Not difficult really. My father always talked about me coming to work in the company, one day to step into his shoes as managing director – that's pretty much all I was ever going to do. It was interesting really. He followed his dream and I suppose he just wanted me to follow it too; his dream of course! I went to sixth form college in Crewe for my A levels (undoubtedly an act of teenage rebellion to move from the strictness of the school regime to the lax day to day life of college!) and then on to Hull University to study Business. After being awarded a degree in Business Management, I did exactly what I had been honed to do and went to work in my father's company upon graduation.

I have to be honest ... working in the photographic industry wasn't really my thing. I slotted neatly into the digital retouching department and spent my days dealing with images in Photoshop and Illustrator and amused myself by doing the odd bit of computer network building but it was never really something you could ever say that I was truly passionate about. Going to work was a chore and leaving at the end of the day was freedom. The only thing that kept me going, day in day out, was the potential to earn money (not that I ever really achieved much of that while I was there!). Ten or so years further down the line and the whole ride came abruptly to an end with the death of my father.

Over that period of time, it's unfortunate to say, the company had slowly come to a tragic death too. Barriers to entry into the photographic industry had steadily fallen from the huge amounts of investment that were required in the 1970s to considerably smaller amounts with the advent of the digital revolution. This meant that individuals working in small industrial units could produce end results that were practically identical to the results we achieved for a fraction of our operating costs. As a company, we still had the running costs of a 22,000 square foot factory and the overheads associated with some 50 plus employees, many of whom had been working for us since the early days. The outcome? The business ceased to trade in 2002 and I found myself at a turning point in my life. Career choice time was on the cards and I was at a crossroads.

Now is probably the right time to tell you that if photography had never been my passion, then music certainly always had. During my university years, I had done a large amount of DJing and a little bit of music production from my basic home studio. In fact I could safely say that it was the only thing that I had ever really enjoyed doing during my life. I spent my days fantasising about working in the music industry. I could see myself, at the Brits ceremony, picking up an award, or in the studio with a band. In my imagination, the studio would be large and luxurious with a vast mixing desk of 120 automated faders stretching out down the room. In front of me was a big glass window, behind which a band would be hammering out one of their tracks. I used to see myself standing in a DJ box, dropping tunes and watching a sea of people dancing with their hands in the air. I could even imagine the buzz I would feel when I saw that crowd going wild in the flashing lights and that close, dark atmosphere of a club when they heard a song that I had produced. I would be thinking "yeah that's mine"! I used to think about this all the time; It was all I ever did think about.

With my options now open, and a little bit of money in the bank, I could wander off down that path if I wanted too and see where the journey would take me. Or I could go into the finance and insurance industry with a friend of mine who was already selling mortgages and the like. Money or passion? Which did I choose? Doh! Money of course! My upbringing had always taught me to follow the money so that's what I did. Now that I think about it, taking that path was the hardest thing I could have done. It felt like I was going against everything I wanted from life; but it felt like I had no choice. My dad had followed his passion but had always ridiculed mine, telling me that 'it wouldn't amount to anything'. My issue was belief. Although I dreamt about music, I never believed it could be my destiny.

And where do you think it got me? I rapidly qualified myself as a financial advisor certified to sell mortgages and insurance. I hardly made any money because I was far too honest and hated every second of it. That's a lesson in itself quite frankly and one that left me feeling pretty much rock bottom in life. I was feeling so bad in fact that Simon invited me to join a course, which he described as something that would 'help me sort my head right out!' I remember it well. We were sat at my sister's wedding and I was telling him about the 'last ten years'. The last time I had seen him was actually during university; a time when my dreams were still fresh. We have talked often since the course and the penny has finally dropped. I have had my 'moment of clarity'. I will come to what that means later.

My passion in life is music and through experience, I now knew that whatever I was going to do I had to feel passionate about it if I was going to succeed. The question was where did I start to give myself the best chance of success? The answer came to me. I was out one day and my girlfriend spotted a billboard poster for an open day at a sound recording college and suggested that I give it a look. Seeing the sign was almost like I was being 'given a sign'. It was hugely coincidental. Fate also dealt a strong hand in the proceedings that followed. The school in question was housed in the same building that had previously been the home of my father's business. I know this because it was me who had sold the school the building five years previously when I liquidated the company. Now I would be going back to somewhere I knew so well and yet hadn't returned to in all that time.

Five days later I walked through the doors of what was, on the outside, a building that had hardly changed, but that on the inside, was unbelievably different. It was fully refurbished and now housed 10 recording studios, 5 different DJ booth setups and its own live venue accommodating up to 250 people. It was perfect in every sense … it would act as a meeting ground for likeminded individuals with whom I could collaborate, whilst also teaching me practically everything that I needed to know about making and producing music. My mind was made up that this course was the way forward for me and now all that I had to do was get accepted onto it. It was mid-August, the course began in early September and it was already fully subscribed at 45 applicants. Not only that, but places were only offered after strict interview by the college principal. Even if I got accepted, it still looked like the earliest I was going to get onto the course would be the following enrolment in March.

Well, now that I had got this far I wasn't going to be put off by anyone or anything. I felt strangely confident. I don't know whether it was because I had seen the light or whether it was the family history with regards to the building. In fact, everything felt right. I made an appointment to see the principal and when I walked through those building doors I felt like nothing was going to stop me getting onto that course. Nothing did stop me. In fact, before I had even had the meeting I was already thinking ahead to what I would have to do next, already believing within myself that I would have a place. I spent five minutes talking to the principal and during that time I convinced him to give me an unconditional offer to start the course that September. Unfortunately, that also meant that one of the existing applicants wouldn't be starting the course, but there was nothing I could do about that, and selfish though that might sound, it wasn't going to stop my determination.

Now, of course, there were other things I had to overcome – not least the issue of money. The course is expensive and I wouldn't be earning any money. I had studied long and hard to qualify as a mortgage advisor and all that work would go to waste. My mum would undoubtedly be concerned and perhaps even disappointed that at 'my age' I appeared to be doing a complete 'about face'. None of that mattered. The only thing that mattered now was my passion. Why? Read on.

The course began in early September and from that point, I can honestly say that I have pushed myself like never before. I knew that if I was to make an impression on the industry and stand a good chance of getting a job that I wanted to do at the end of the course (especially when the majority of my fellow students were considerably younger than me), then nothing short of excellence would get me to that point. More importantly, for the first time in my life, I truly believed that I could achieve that. Confidence and determination were not emotions that had featured strongly thus far in my life, but all of a sudden I had them both in bucket-loads.

The first exam that I took was approximately 3 months after starting and it had a pass mark of 90%. High some might say, but then in an industry where so many people want to work and so few 'cut the mustard', an easy pass would have been pointless and would count for nothing. Forty five people sat the exam and 3 people passed. I achieved a first time score of 94%, making me one of those three. Since then I have produced similar achievements with projects and further exams, each time succeeding I'm sure because of my fundamental belief that nothing would stop me or beat me.

I love the quote by Thomas Wolfe: **"You have reached the pinnacle of success as soon as you become uninterested in money, compliments, or publicity."** *Passion over money, ladies and gentlemen.*

I can honestly say that I don't recall a point in my life where my income has been so low and yet I have never been happier. Whatever the future has in store for me, I know that it's going to come from this path and, more importantly, I know that I am not going to stop until I am really good at it!

So, all this is very well, but what was this moment of clarity that I spoke of? Why did I suddenly start to achieve? Why did I suddenly about face and go after this passion of mine with no game plan? Why am I so driven? Why did I pluck up the courage to tell my mum that the sensible job I had, along with all the work I had done towards it, was going in the bin? Why? What changed between the old me and the new me?

I began to believe in the beauty of my dream (as I think Eleanor Roosevelt once said) rather than ignoring it. I realised that I had been doing the hard work for years. I had been dreaming about this all my life! My moment of clarity was simply to stop thinking of it as a 'castle in the air' and start to think about it in reality. All I did was stop fantasising about it and start to believe it was possible. All my life I had kept on coming back to music but had let the barriers dominate my mind; I just stopped allowing that to happen.

The amazing thing has been that it was the easiest decision I have ever made. Working so hard has never been so effortless and I have never been so happy. In fact I never imagined I could be so happy. It is a weight off my shoulders. Why has it been so easy? Because I have done all the dreaming I ever needed to do. I have been building a pathway in my brain towards music all my life. I was an expert at this stuff without even knowing it. I just needed to be told how to direct those dreams properly.

What is so special about Nick's story? Nothing, and that is why it is *so special*. The fact that so many people who read it can relate to it. How many of you are now thinking, 'how on earth did I end up in the job I am in?' How many of you are thinking, 'it certainly wasn't out of passion'. Many people have been fantasising like Nick all their lives. Isn't it time to turn those fantasies into DayDreams, just as Nick did?

Was it a coincidence that he saw the sign for the music school at the time he did? No. The belief he gained in his fantasy turned it into a DayDream. The pathway in his brain became his 'path of least resistance'. His brain then began to look for opportunities. The sign happened to be the first opportunity that presented itself. Rather than dismissing it as 'too hard' and 'just a pipe dream', Nick then followed through with action – action that was driven by his DayDream.

Write down here some of the things that you have dismissed as fantasy in the past. Maybe not all of them could be turned into DayDreams. Maybe, just maybe some of them could…

Notes

Notes

RuleSeven
YouCan't
KidAKidder

7

Your DayDream must be believable to you.

This is the difference between day dreaming as we know it and DayDreaming as we are redefining it. This is the crux of Nick's story.

The dream must be believable to you. By this I mean the brain has to accept it as a picture of truth. If you perceive it as fantastical then it will remain just that, a fantasy. The whole point of setting this goal and picturing the dream is to build the belief in it. Building belief is about quietening down the doubting voices in your head. If that doubting voice is too strong, then unfortunately your brain is getting two signals – a positive and a negative.

One positive and one negative equal nothing.

I always think of the old Tom and Jerry cartoons with this rule. Do you remember when Tom the cat used to chase Jerry around the kitchen? Every now and then, Jerry would spin around a corner and duck under a piece of menacingly solid furniture. You knew what was coming. Tom would fly around the corner, too fast to stop in time and too tall to avoid it. WHAM! Tom would be knocked to the ground. His whole body would shudder as if he were a piece of wood rattling under the impact. As he then lay unconscious on the black and white tiled floor under the table, two figures would float above his head. They would usually take the feline form of a devil and an angel, the angel telling him how 'good' he is and encouraging him not to eat that poor little mouse called Jerry. Of course, the devil would tell Tom about the pleasures of such an activity, reminding him how tasty this would be and how satisfied he would feel afterwards. The 'voice of his conscience' would battle it out in a winner takes all fight for the undisputed crown and control of Tom's behaviour.

When thinking about goals and dreams, imagine the doubting voices as this little devil on your shoulder. Design and develop these dreams in a way that gives the devil no corner to hide in. You need to knock him clean out of the ring!

If I want to race in Formula 1. I could imagine myself driving around Monaco, dicing with the greatest drivers at high speed. However, if I don't *believe* that this could actually happen, if the doubting voices that rage in my head afterwards outweigh my dream, then I am getting nowhere. Bob Geldof is reported to have described this as the "civil war in your head." You must win this war.

Example: **Say what you mean**

This always reminds me of a great story that split the believers from those who simply 'say they believe'. Charles

Blondin walked on a tightrope from the top of Niagara Falls down to Goat Island – 1000 feet there and then back – in the wind and rain, with the rope swaying a reported 90 feet each way. He asked the crowd if they believed he could do it. They sang in unison "we believe!" On completion of this amazing feat, the crowd chanted his name and cheered his skill and bravery. He asked the crowd if they believed he could now re trace those very steps, this time though, with someone sitting on his shoulders. They shouted as one, with the evidence firmly in place in their mind "we believe!"

He asked for a volunteer.

You guessed it. None of them believed quite enough to put themselves forward. Suddenly the doubting voices crept in and impeded their behaviour. It is these voices we must avoid or overcome.

If you look at Wayne's example from earlier in this book, there were many doubters. Often these doubters were so called experts who 'just knew' he couldn't and wouldn't do it. There was only ONE person that knew he could and would. That one person was all it needed – Wayne himself. Only he knew what the voices in his head were saying about this dream of his. To be more accurate, only he had any control over the voices.

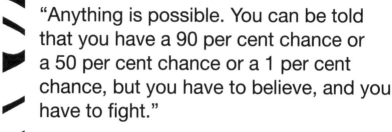

"Anything is possible. You can be told that you have a 90 per cent chance or a 50 per cent chance or a 1 per cent chance, but you have to believe, and you have to fight."

LANCE ARMSTRONG

There are a number of ways in which you can help yourself to create a believable DayDream.

1. Make sure the picture is within YOUR belief threshold.

I highlight the word 'your' here because that is the only belief threshold you need to answer to. There are many pictures you can paint for the same goal. It is the picture that needs to be believable. If you want to run your first marathon, then picturing the clock at the finishing line with a world record time upon it may be beyond your capabilities and beliefs. Perhaps a different picture of the time on that clock would be more advisable. That belief threshold will be different from goal to goal and from person to person, but only you know whether it is a stretch too far for your imagination.

2. Set interim DayDreams to build towards the huge audacious goal.

You can help yourself with DayDreams along the way if the end result seems just too much for you to swallow in one mouthful. You can form a picture for key milestone along the way, which will drive you towards each step. Seeing yourself at the top of Everest may be more believable if you can also see yourself at the top of other, less challenging mountains that build up to the ultimate climb. As you achieve those milestones, then your picture at the top of Everest will become ever more real to you.

Sometimes those milestones will be easier to define than others. My sister Mandy set herself a DayDream to become a black belt in a form of kickboxing. The different coloured belts along the way give her natural markers to aim for along the way.

In the last chapter we talked about the importance of performance goals as well as outcome goals and how the two can be combined. You can write separate performance related DayDreams that mark your progress along the way, keeping your final outcome or main DayDream in mind to give your behaviours the right overall direction.

3. Make sure you give yourself enough time.

If in doubt, make sure that your target date gives you plenty of time to achieve the goal. This can help with the believability of your inspirational dream. Building your dream house in two weeks could well be asking too much, even for the most faithful of individuals (of course, it depends on the house!). However, giving yourself a year makes this dream seem more plausible.

Example: **Writing a Book**

I have a friend who wanted to write a book. By his own admission he is not the most patient of people, and the thought of him sitting still for anything more than about ten minutes at a time and concentrating on one thing was not only far fetched, it was a frankly unattractive proposition.

He told me that, whilst trying to get a clear picture of his inspirational dream, based around finishing the entire book, all he could hear in his head were doubting voices. As we discovered early in this book, all those doubting voices were doing was pointing his behaviour towards the hurdles that he was focusing on.

Hurdles such as:

"You don't have the time."

"You don't have the patience!"

"Only clever people write books and you failed English!"

The problem was, in trying to imagine the entire book written, he was going beyond his current belief threshold. He came up with a great idea. In order to help himself make that dream more believable to him, he wrote a series of daydreams that told the story at different stages of his goal. He broke it down into bite size pieces, whilst still focusing on creating DayDreams about those bite size pieces. The temptation when a goal is broken down is to focus on the tasks. Keep your mind on the outcomes along the way rather than the tasks.

For example: He wrote down the story of finishing his first chapter, just 10 pages long. He described the scene just two weeks into the future:

"It is 31st August and I am sat at my desk, listening to the printer reel off the first ten pages of my book. As I pop the cork on a miniature bottle of champagne, I take the sheets from the tray and begin to read my work. As I sip, the bubbles go up my nose. I toast my first chapter."

Because this picture was within his belief threshold and the doubting voices failed to dominate his mind, his behaviour followed his dream, rather than getting stuck in the barriers to it. With one chapter written, he believed that the second was within his grasp. With more written along the way, this drove him, stage by stage, to get the thing written.

He linked this to the overall DayDream, set 9 months into the future:

"It is May 10th, my mother's birthday, and I am sat in my parent's kitchen. I sign one of the 200 books I have had printed especially for friends and family, and to send to selected publishers. This is the first edition, copy number 1, and I sign the

inside cover, "to my greatest inspiration. Mum n Dad". I hope they are proud."

This picture was believable to him. I imagine that if he had seen himself receiving the Nobel Prize for literature, the doubting voices may well have reared their ugly heads!

Looking at my own goal to be a Formula 1 racing driver, I only need to look as far as Mike's story from the pages of this book for inspiration. Mike was 'creative' with his dream because he had to be. He won't mind me saying that his best footballing years are past him, and yet he still found a way to *'live his dream'*. I am sure I could find a way to *'live my dream'* creatively. I could race other classes, drive an F1car on a test day, or work in Formula 1 in some other way. Only I know which answer will satisfy my desire. Only I know how far I need to go.

There may of course be some DayDreams that are genuinely impossible. I mentioned this briefly earlier in the book. What if someone who wanted a child, and was struggling to do so, went through all this process to drive themselves to it, and then found out that they were physically incapable? Well, firstly, miracles do happen, and of course they will only ever have a child if they are doing the right things! My eldest sister spent 7 years dreaming of a second child. That vision, I have no doubt, drove Debbie to put herself through immense physical and mental pain in order to achieve her goal. Those behaviours came as a result of DayDreaming.

However, miracles may not always happen in the way that people first envisage them. Sometimes there are limits that cannot be overcome. It is then that true DayDreams come into their own. There are many ways to achieve a goal. My sister could have gone down a number of routes to have her second child. From treatment to surrogacy; from the use of a donor to adoption; your ability to make your picture believable enables you to achieve your ultimate goal by several means.

The dream needs only to be believable to you. Set audacious goals. Remember, what seems audacious to one person may be simple to another.

TopTips

- **Give yourself enough time**
- **Set interim DayDreams**
- **Keep the picture real to you**
- **Be creative with your dreams**

Achieving any goal needs work. There are potential problems, effort to put in, preparation, hard work, commitment and more. These barriers in our mind can be real or imagined, it doesn't matter.

Think of a simple goal you would like to achieve – nothing fancy. Clearing out the garage, putting up some shelves, making a fabulous three course meal, it really doesn't matter. Write this down below – put it into the form of a DayDream to practise the process.

Now, think about all the things you will have to 'do' in order to realise this dream.

These are the 'real' problems. The things that people see as being the barriers to them achieving their goals. These are the things that you must do in order to bring your 'dream' into reality.

Now, imagine and write down some of the 'potential' problems you may have. These problems could include anything that might jeopardise you achieving your goal but may not actually happen. Be as creative as you want to be!

These are the 'potential' or imagined problems, those that may not necessarily happen. However, just the thought of them is enough to put you off trying to achieve the goal at all.

All of these problems, whether real or imagined, are directing you away from your DayDream.

In order to set an effective goal, one that works for us, one that will actually drive us to achieve rather than see us write it off as just another unfulfilled 'New Year's Resolution', we have to get our imagination onto the DayDream behind our goal. This stops us focusing on the problems that will in turn stop us achieving.

It is this that enables us to build the belief needed to continually drive our behaviours towards our goal.

Exercise: **Keep your eyes on the ball**

We need to remember to 'keep our eye on the ball'. Try this out with some more of your own examples below.

Exercise: Keep your eyes on the ball

"Dreams at first seem impossible, then they seem improbable, and then, when we summon the will, they soon become inevitable."

CHRISTOPHER REEVE

RuleEight
ANeedTo
KnowBasis

8

You CAN keep them secret if you really want to.

Only tell people about your dreams if you really trust them. Everyone has what can only be described as 'toxic friends'. Although they may masquerade as positive influences, actually they do just the opposite.

These toxic friends will do what they always do best – talk you down.

"You!? Fly in a hot air balloon over the Serengeti Plains? You're afraid of heights aren't you?

"You!? Star in a play? You've always been as quiet as a mouse! What about all the time in rehearsals?"

"You!? Start your own business? What if it goes wrong? What about the impact on your family?"

We have heard it all before, haven't we? There are many reasons why someone would do this. It makes them feel superior, powerful, in control and keeps you on THEIR level. As soon as you achieve anything in life, it makes them feel small.

It isn't always through pure cynicism that people behave this way though. Much of the time, their discouraging words come as a result of their lack of self belief, their perception that they couldn't do it. Of course, as far as they are concerned, if they can't, then no-one can.

Remember, the school bully is often the most insecure person in the playground.

Wayne described how the so called experts in cycling told him that he wouldn't be able to cycle the Alps. This was negative influence that Wayne didn't need. As he proved, it can be overcome. My view is – 'why make it any harder than it already is?'

Example: **Fifteen minutes from glory**

A few years ago I set a DayDream to help me run The London Marathon. Long distance running was not my favourite pastime. I was likely to be the kid in school who took the shortcut on cross country day. I knew therefore I would need a really strong picture to help me achieve this goal. I needed a DayDream.

The goal was to run the London Marathon.

My DayDream was as follows:

"It is April 18th 2004 and I am just crossing the finish line of The London Marathon. With Buckingham Palace behind me I finish strongly, arms in the air as I look up at the clock and drink in the time. 3:58:06. I have done it! I have finished in less than 4 hours! The crowd is applauding and my legs feel like lead. As I stop to collect my medal, people pat me on the back. My

*legs want to continue moving and they go all shaky. They hand
me the foil space blanket and I wrap it around me proudly and
walk in the sunshine, head held high with a bottle of water in my
hand. I spot my wife in the crowd of waiting people and try to
run to her…we giggle as my legs fail to get going!"*

This was my DayDream, the picture I imagined everyday.
This drove me to train, raise money, sign up for the race and
ultimately run it. There is an interesting little sub story though. I
didn't quite meet my time commitment in the picture. I told many
people about this dream. It was amazing how many people were
prepared to tell me that running a marathon in under four hours,
given I had never run the distance before, would be too much.
This was not cynicism; this was purely their limiting beliefs being
manifested through words. Eventually I made the fatal error
of listening to them. I changed the time in my DayDream from
3:58:06 to 4:28:06 to make it more *realistic*.

I had pictured myself for three months running in under 4
hours, then spent the next three months leading up to the race
picturing my finish a half hour later.

I ran the race in just under 4 hours and fifteen minutes –
slap bang in between.

Your brain is a powerful thing. Be careful who you allow to
influence it.

There are, however, some people who will need to know. If this DayDream involves others, it would be a great idea to include them! Often we keep our goals secret from others who are close to us for fear of disappointing them when we don't achieve it. This is a reflection of our fear of falling short.

Telling those people close to you is often a great sign of commitment born out of a strong belief in your ability to achieve it. It can also, therefore, help to generate this commitment, should you choose to let those people in on the secret.

They will do a number of things for you. They will encourage you; they will support you; they may 'kick you' into action; they might even do it with you! So with these people:

 "Talk about a dream – try to make it real."
BRUCE SPRINGSTEEN

My wife wanted to begin a photography business. She had always been interested in photography but had never really believed that anyone else would be interested in her photography. She had thought about this for some time and dreamt about an exhibition or a gallery where her work would be shown to people.

A few close friends encouraged her to act on it. Shortly after, she had a phone call from one of those very same friends who had asked in a restaurant whether they would be interested in exhibiting her work. They had jumped at the chance to have free wall decorations and had agreed to allow the pictures to be sold direct from their wall!

Just a couple of years later, Laurie has her exhibition and has sold nearly 100 photographs. She has lived her dream and continues to do so. Would it have happened without her friend? I am sure it would, perhaps just in a different way. There are many routes to a destination remember. This just happens to be the route that proved best for Laurie. Sometimes, that really is what friends are for!

TopTips

- **Keep your DayDreams out of the reach of toxic friends**
- **Put up a mental shield to anyone who tries to discourage you. It's YOUR dream after all!**
- **Tell those people you trust. Support can be a good thing**

"You should nurse your dreams and protect them through bad times and tough times to the sunshine and light which always comes."

WOODROW WILSON

Come fly with me...

**Neil
Osgood**

"It is August 2007 – We've spent a lovely day by the pool, splashing around with the boys. All four of us are now sitting around the table in a local restaurant in Spain and ready to order our evening meal. We've all got huge smiles on our lightly tanned faces and as the warm Mediterranean sun drops behind the horizon, the waiter approaches to take our order."

After taking my first flight at the age of 16 to Spain with a friend and his family, I had been on between 30 or 40 flights to a variety of destinations ranging from France to Mexico with no mishaps. All this changed when I took a short trip to Holland with my wife.

Amanda and I had been married for three years and prior to our children coming along we had always 'treated' ourselves to a little city break on our anniversary each September. In 1998, we decided on Amsterdam as our venue and went about booking the trip and thinking about what we would do whilst over there. The outbound flight was perfect and we thoroughly enjoyed our four day break taking in the canals, museums and trips out to The Hague and Rotterdam. The excitement happened on our journey back home.

Despite flying many times previously, I had always been uneasy about it and usually this was highlighted during take off, but then subsided during the remainder of the flight. As we set off from Amsterdam it was a perfect autumnal day and, as usual, I was a little on edge as we took off. As we got to cruising altitude the fear didn't go away and I realised I was on the edge of having a panic attack. Although being extremely frightened I managed to calm myself down and with the short tenure of the flight (40 minutes) I managed to make it to the landing *without any major incidents. Although I didn't realise this at the time, this was to have a major impact on me longer term.*

Six months later we booked a holiday to Grenada (in the Caribbean) which was an eight hour flight. With the previous incident fresh in my mind I decided to take medical advice and was given some mild sedatives to take during the flights. The experience was awful and although we had a fantastic holiday, during both flights I sat there like a 'rabbit in headlights' for eight hours, clinging on for grim death. NEVER AGAIN – and so it proved, at least for a while, as I didn't board a plane again for eight years!!!!!

A few years later we were blessed with the arrival of our 2 little boys – Samuel (who at the time of writing is 6) and Isaac (who is 4). Both my wife and I had agreed that when the children were little we didn't want to take them overseas due to the challenge of carrying all the equipment etc. in addition to the worry if they became ill at some stage. We agreed to consider holidaying abroad once again when our youngest came to around 4 or 5, which constituted a 'get out of jail free card' for me.

Separate to this, I had changed jobs in 2000 and moved from a career in banking into an accountancy firm. It was there that I met one of the partners, Jacqui Chatwood, who I would eventually work for. Jacqui was going to have a major impact on my life even though I didn't know it at the time. After 6 months, Jacqui left the business and began working for one of her clients, Advance Performance. We kept in contact over the next couple of years and in May 2004, Jacqui asked me to come and join the team – I didn't hesitate for a second!!

One of the major elements of my induction into Advance was

to attend an Open Programme and learn about all that they teach.
Simon worked for Advance at that time and he ran the programme. The
impact was immediate, this was the moment where I knew I was going
to change the way I viewed my life in the future. I had always been a bit
of a pessimist and the material and ideas were ground breaking for me. I
remember feeling as if a light had switched on in the recesses of my brain
and everything somehow became clear.

With a new found spring in my step, I undertook a review of my
life. One thing that became very clear was my desire to travel and see a
great deal of the world. Of course, this meant confronting my challenges
with flying – this is when I put together my inspirational DayDream.

After not even being able to look at pictures of the inside of a
plane without my heartbeat doubling in pace, I began rebuilding my
confidence. My initial action was to write down my dream to paint a solid
picture in my head as to what I wanted to experience with my family. I
carried these thoughts around with me everyday, as well as a written
version in my wallet. Thinking about it time and time again, I could feel
the desire welling up inside me, as well as the belief that this was not just
a possibility – this was an inevitability.

The next challenge was deciding how I would make this become
a reality.

I decided to get some extra help and actually went to see a
hypnotherapist. This, I have to say, is very unusual behaviour for me. I
would have considered that to be very extreme and to be honest, would
have doubted the effectiveness of it. However, my mind was open and
I was happy to try anything! He agreed to help me out with a couple of

sessions. These went fantastically well and helped me to start building my confidence. I began to think much more comfortably about stepping aboard a plane. I started to talk to myself about how excited my kids would be the first time they boarded a plane and how much I would enjoy the experience. I could picture their little faces glowing as we boarded and set off on our exciting journey.

The only negative I was having at this time was my trepidation about appearing to be scared in front of my children and subsequently passing on my fear to them. In reaction to these thoughts, I now knew that the most effective way to tackle this would be to look at the option of taking a flight, to tackle it 'head on', however scared I was. After making some enquiries, I came across a company that ran a programme called "Fear of Flying". All of this, up until now, I had kept quiet as I didn't want to get my kids or wife all excited about a holiday, only for me to back out at the last minute through fear. Therefore, it was now time for the ultimate commitment. I chatted about the flying programmes to my wife. She desperately wanted to book a family holiday, so was really excited. I relaxed, thinking that she would suggest I attend the course nearer to us in Manchester, which was a couple of months away. She plunged in, encouraging me to sign up straight away and get along to the course in a couple of weeks in Newcastle. Ironically, I grew up in Newcastle and spent many happy hours at the airport with my granddad, watching the planes land. Telling my wife had given me more impetus than I had ever had and I agreed to go to this earlier course. Where I had kept this a secret before for fear of upsetting those involved if I didn't carry it through, I now knew that this was it – there was no going back. Involving those I loved was the ultimate motivation.

A few weeks later, I packed my things and said an emotional goodbye to my wife and the boys. The tears were streaming down my eyes as I drove north, but I knew that this was going to allow us to do great things in the future. The programme went really well, with a 747 Captain providing details of what happens on a plane from the cockpit. We then had a talk from the head of cabin crew training about all the safeguards and procedures the crew have to go through to allow us to fly safely. The sessions were really informative and put my mind at ease and, before we knew it, we were heading over to the airport to take a 45 minute flight in the skies of the North East.

After going through customs we settled ourselves in the departure lounge, ready to set off. All the delegates were in the same boat (or should I say plane!) as me and every single one of us was on a knife edge. We then received the news that our flight would be delayed and we wouldn't be boarding for another 90 minutes. The atmosphere changed amongst everyone and I rang my wife for some comfort. I was incredibly nervous but, after having a conversation with her, I understood and reinforced why I was there. I was ready.

We boarded the plane and I took my seat, the realisation that my issues were minor to some other people hit me full on. There were some delegates who couldn't enter the plane and some others who were frightened out of their 'wits'. Eventually we took off and, amongst screams and other sounds, I couldn't believe it – I was so relaxed. During the flight I managed to read a copy of the in-flight magazine and actually enjoyed the time. I surprised myself on our descent by looking out of the *window as we approached the airport. We landed safely then exited the aircraft and, as we travelled back to the terminal, what I'd achieved hit me. After fearing to go near a plane and even an airport for 8 years, I'd now turned it all around. It would be an understatement to say that I had a big smile on my face. I didn't get home until the following morning as it was so late by the time I left. It didn't bother me. I could have fuelled my car home with the energy this had given me.*

Upon returning home, my wife immediately seized the opportunity and booked our first family holiday – we were all going to Spain. Over the coming weeks the build up was brilliant, encouraging the boys to learn some basic Spanish words and going shopping with them for holiday clothes. Soon enough, the day of departure (30th July 2007) came along. The children were so excited, asking every 5 minutes, "when are we flying dad, when are we flying?" As we went through passport control and down to the gate, my stomach was starting to churn, but one look down at my boys, along with picturing my dream again soon calmed me down.

A short while later we were called to board the plane and the boys were jumping around like popcorn. We sat in our seats and got settled in whilst waiting for take off. I giggled to myself as I watched both of them. They were so small they could sit crossed legs in the seats. Isaac, my youngest (who has the reputation of a bit of a chatterbox), was sitting next to a lovely lady who he was avidly chatting away with, telling her that he was going to Spain in an aeroplane up in the sky – it was so sweet!!! As soon as we starting moving, my eldest son, Sam, who I was sitting next to, asked if we were in the sky yet. I explained that as soon as we were, he would know. Whilst waiting at the end of the runway, I was getting a little nervous and Sam looked up at me and said, "Dad – this is so exciting" and his little face was absolutely glowing – I will remember this picture in my mind's eye forever. At this point all my hang ups disappeared and I sat back completely relaxed, ready for our holiday.

The flight was great, with Sam and me playing a couple of games together and listening to music. We regularly looked out of the window and Sam pointed out the land down below and the beautiful views of the clouds. On the other side of the aisle, both my wife and Isaac slept for the majority of the flight. As we came into land two and a half hours later, everyone was in high spirits. After going through passport control we went to collect our luggage and, as we sat down together at the carousel, Amanda and I looked at each other knowingly. "Yes – we've done it," you could hear us both say, and we had a huge group hug.

The following ten days were pure heaven and fulfilled the expectations I had pictured in my mind. We went swimming with our children in the pool and took bus journeys into the local town, which brought back fantastic memories of previous holidays abroad some 7 or 8 years ago.

The most enjoyable and memorable part of the holiday was the first evening my family spent abroad together. We'd had a fantastic day in the sun and the boys were so full of energy after spending most of the time playing with me in the pool. After a short siesta at teatime, we all showered, and put on smart clothes and set off for something to eat. All our faces were beaming and we were joking with each other as we walked. I looked at the 3 faces beside me and felt a well of emotion rise up about our achievement; my achievement.

As we came to what became the boy's favourite restaurant, 'Grumbles', we pulled our chairs up to our table. We sat down and the waitress walked over - I started to think "I've seen this picture somewhere before!"

Neil's story demonstrates that we can use positive pictures to overcome fears and phobias. He kept his DayDream a secret, for fear of disappointing people around him. Once he told those he loved and trusted, once he involved them, it appears there was no holding him back! Sometimes other people can provide the catalyst.

Neil undertook hypnotherapy to help himself achieve his DayDream. He says himself that this course of action was something he had never imagined he would take. Taking hypnotherapy is a behaviour to achieve a goal, driven by that all-consuming vision of it. Think about times when you have done things that were out of character in order to achieve a goal.

It's a great example of a *negative goal,* such as a phobia or bad habit that you would like to break. Neil wanted to *avoid* the fear of flying. He used positive hooks to picture the result he wanted and lived his dream!

Relate this story to some of your fears and habits and jot down your thoughts opposite.

Notes

RuleNine
WalkThe
Tightrope

9

Keep your goals balanced.

At any one time, you might have a few daydreams on the go. How many is really your choice. How many do you feel comfortable with? How many can you manage at the same time? How many do you believe you can handle?

How ever many you do have, please make sure they are balanced. You should concentrate on the different areas of your life that are important to you. If you write them about only one thing, then that is the only thing you will go after. If that is good for you, then who am I to judge? However, be aware that there are many examples from history where obsession for just one thing, be it money, success in work, love or fitness, can lead to the exclusion of other important things.

You and ONLY you know what is important to you. You can apply DayDreaming to anything. This book is written in such a way that I hope it sparks many ideas for its use. I have tried to give many examples, and the stories have been picked out from many others to do just that.

We have all read and heard many disaster stories of people who have achieved fantastic things in one area of their life, but that has come at the cost of others. George Best is one example that comes to mind.

You can write DayDreams about an infinite number of subjects (although my advice would be to start with a few to get you going!)

As well as balancing the subject matter, spreading the timescales of your different DayDreams is important too. Have short term, medium term and long term DayDreams. This enables you to spread them over time, rather than feel under pressure to progress on many things simultaneously. If you have 5 written and they all aim towards one date, this will undoubtedly make things more difficult come the time!

It is at this point that the subject of values crops up. Which areas of your life do you value? How do you want to live your life? How do you ensure that you don't harm others in order to achieve your goals? How do you ensure that the methods you use to get there are not to your detriment? The ultimate example of this is sports people who turn to performance enhancing drugs. One could say that their DayDream is so strong that they are prepared to turn to any method to achieve it. Personal values are therefore important in helping you to achieve your goals in 'the right way' – whatever that is. That is the subject of a whole other book, but still worth thinking about when creating DayDreams.

TopTips

- Write DayDreams that cover the 5 most important areas in your life
- Once you begin to doubt you have the time for them all, you should probably avoid writing anymore, until you have achieved some
- Balance DayDreams in terms of timescales

The following exercise is great fun and is inspired by the original Life List writer, the one and only John Goddard. When he was 15 years old, John wrote a list of goals – 127 to be exact. He categorised them into different areas and set about achieving as many as he could in his lifetime. By the time he was in his mid 70s he had completed 109 of his goals. Amazing! He is known as 'the real life Indiana Jones' – my hero. By creating your own list, taking into account lots of different areas, you will have many goals to use as the basis for writing DayDreams, and this will ensure that your list is balanced.

Let your head run free. They can be big or small. They can be for next week or for ten years time. In fact a good mix is the best way. This is just a list for inspiration. Have fun!

Choose categories from the following list:

Places to go	Things to do
Skills to learn	Things to achieve
People to meet	Finance
Career	Home
Health	Sport
Music	Recreation and Hobbies
Family	Friends

Exercise: **Life List**

Use these categories to think about the different goals you would like to achieve. Write a list of goals under each. Include some in each category – the more you find you write in one area, the more important that area is to you. Just ensure that you are keeping some balance. Add other categories too if you feel I have missed one!

Exercise: **Life List**

"Be careful what you wish for; you are likely to get it."

CHRISTOPHER MARLOWE'S DR. FAUSTUS

RuleTen
ThePen
IsMightier

...

10

Write your DayDreams down.

I have read that at Harvard Business School, the graduating class of 1954 was asked a number of questions as part of their exit interview. Two particular questions were to have great significance for the world of personal and organisational development.

Question 1: how many of you here can honestly say that you have well defined goals for your life after college?

10% of the year group answered that they could honestly say they did have well defined goals for their future.

Question 2: those of you that do have well defined goals – how many of you intend to write them down and regularly review them?

Just under half of those people that had well defined goals said that they intended to write them down and regularly review them – around 4% of the total year group.

Twenty years later, Harvard gathered together as many of the group as they could for a reunion. This was not simply an excuse for a few beers. They saw it as a research opportunity.

They ascertained the financial success of the group. Admittedly, not everyone in the world thinks of success as purely monetary, but many people believe that it is, rightly or wrongly, a marker for much of society.

Incredibly, they found the 10% of the group that had well defined goals were individually ALL within the highest quartile in terms of annual earnings/salary.

Astoundingly, they found that the 4% of the group that had committed to writing those goals down and regularly reviewing them were collectively worth more (in financial terms) than the other 96% PUT TOGETHER!

It's not scientific evidence; it's not hard and fast proof. However, I see it as a rather unceremonious shove towards the fact that…

WRITING your DayDreams down, then visualising them, gives you a greater chance of actually achieving them. Writing them out will keep you from becoming lazy with the rules in the rest of this book. The process of actually putting them down on paper will make you think about them more carefully, more deeply and, most importantly, more effectively. Best of all, if you write them down, you have the pleasure of looking back at the written goal when you have achieved it. You can revel in the fact that you can see when and how you set the goal, how you started to make it happen rather than just feeling like it happened to you.

How you choose to write them down is personal to you. Some people prefer to describe the DayDream in all its glory on paper as well as in their mind. Some people choose to write down a few key words or even just one word that acts as a trigger for the entire picture.

I strongly encourage you to keep your DayDreams on cards. That way, you can keep them to hand more easily. The cards themselves can then be used as a reminder of the goal.

Pens at the ready please!

TopTips

- **Write down the DayDream, or something that triggers the DayDream, not just the goal**
- **Use cards to write them down**
- **Keep the cards in a place you will see them often e.g. in your car or on the fridge door!**

"The pen is mightier than the sword."

CHARLIE CHAPLIN

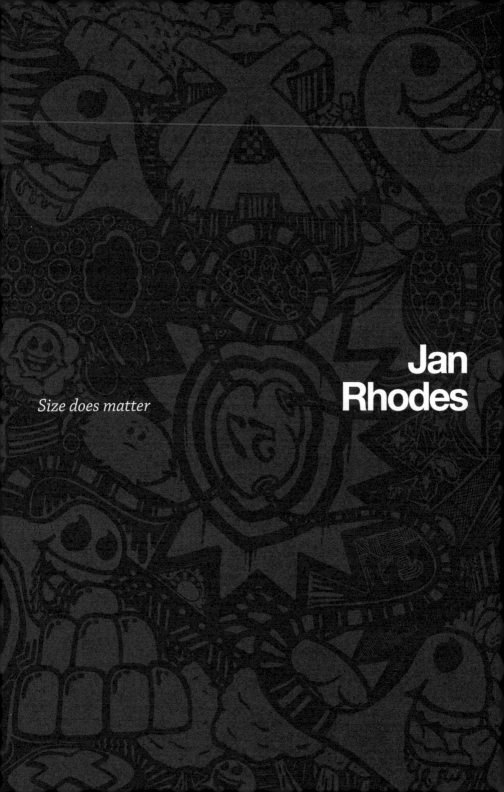

Size does matter

**Jan
Rhodes**

To say that I was overweight as a child is an understatement. By the time I was two years old, I was tall, big-boned, and chubby. In the fourth grade I weighed as much as my teacher. In the sixth grade, people thought I was my father's wife because I was so big (I was 5'7" tall and wore a size 16 dress). When I was thirteen I remember visiting the doctor's office for medication to speed up my metabolism. My teenage years were difficult. I tried every conceivable type of diet but nothing worked – it was a roller coaster of ups and downs.

At age 22, I was engaged to be married and at the time wore a size 18 dress. In preparation for our wedding I stopped eating (literally) so that I could lose weight to fit into a "small" wedding gown. I got down to a size 12 but I was fainting and not losing weight in a healthy, safe way. For that one moment in time, however, I was a size 12 – an event not repeated since.

Shortly after my wedding, I gained everything back and then some. That's when I just gave up. I told myself that I was born to be fat. "I had inherited fat genes from my grandmothers and there was simply nothing that I could do about it. I would never diet again!"

And, for all intents and purposes, I kept that goal in my mind. Until, of course, my health began to suffer. At age 40, I had a life-threatening illness that was brought on by my obesity. The doctor told me that I had to lose weight otherwise my illness would escalate. I dieted for 8 months, and when my health was restored, I went back to the old patterns and habits for the next 14 years. I knew that at some point my life-long history of obesity would catch up to me, but there was nothing I could do to prevent it – at least that's what I thought.

At the age of 53, I was a size 22/24. I had high blood pressure, Type II diabetes, shortness of breath and heart palpitations. My back ached constantly; my knees were always in pain. I would sleep for only a few hours each night and then lie awake wondering how much longer I would live because I felt my health was beyond repair. I gave up eating sweets to compensate for the diabetes and so I lost a few pounds, but nothing significant.

I made a decision to find a new doctor who could help me – one that focused on metabolism and endocrinology. I was sure that by now he would have a magic pill – the key to losing weight quickly and easily.

My first visit confirmed everything I thought. My health was out of control. I now was a size 26. The doctor told me that if I continued on the path that I had been following all these years, he was sure I would not live to be an old woman and enjoy life with my husband and family. He also told me that all of my health problems were as a result of my obesity and that if I lost weight my health would improve considerably. These were not the words I wanted to hear. He had no miracle cure. He was telling me that I had a lot of work to do.

I remember thinking that the doctor had no idea how hard this was going to be. Why? I had been fat all my life. I couldn't change how I lived, how I ate, how the gene pool affected me! But I really had no choice. I loved my family and I loved my life. I had a wonderful husband, a great son, lots of friends, a super career, a nice home.

As much as I tried to think otherwise, I was convinced that I would not be successful. But, to appease the doctor, I would give it a go. If past history was any indication, this would be a temporary situation.

When my health improved, I could go off my diet. I decided to count calories and get this "temporary situation" moving forward.

It worked – for the first three weeks. I lost 14 pounds. This was great. If I could keep losing at that rate it would not take long at all. Now, of course, I deluded myself that this would be easy. My body set me straight very quickly. In the fourth and fifth weeks of my calorie counting, faithfully staying on track and starving myself, I didn't lose an ounce. Depression set in and I was angry. Excuse after excuse set in. I convinced myself that I couldn't do it – there was no way I could succeed. But I promised I'd give it one more week so that I could at least tell the doctor I tried.

At the end of that week (the sixth week on 1200 calories a day) I actually gained four pounds. I was told that my body thought it was starving to death so it was trying to preserve me. Now, really, if you had seen me at that time you would have been well assured that I was not starving to death!

At this time I attended a programme. I was sceptical and ready to show it! I had just gained weight when dieting for goodness sake. The last thing I needed was to be sent by my company onto a programme that talked about achieving goals. I had tried and failed and that was that.

What I learned knocked me cold. My problem was that I'd always focused on the task and not the goal. I was obsessed with the numbers and not the reason behind them! Desire was the key to success. If I could picture what I wanted, it would drive me to remarkable results, despite temporary defeats.

Immediately, a mental picture of what I wanted to achieve came to mind. It was an old photograph of me, at that one moment in time, when I was a size 12. I saw it, I felt it, and I was living that moment again. That was my goal – to fit into the dress I was wearing in the photo, a dress that for some reason I had kept tucked away in an old trunk in the closet for all these years. It was all up to me and I had the power to make changes in my life.

I still remember the words now: "When your dream is more powerful than the obstacle, you will make it happen." That did it. I started dreaming and did not stop. I could not get the picture out of my mind. I knew that it was going to take work but as long as I focused on my goal, I would handle the tasks one at a time. It was now August, 2001. My goal was to lose 110 pounds in a year. My dream was to stand in that dress!

Counting calories wasn't the way for me to go so I joined a "diet management program" and began eating in a healthy, balanced manner. I was eating more than on the previous crash diet and I was losing weight. This was a plan I could live with for the rest of my life. My body was not always cooperative, but I started losing an average of 4 to 5 pounds a month. I was concerned because at that rate it would take me longer than my target of 'within a year', but I kept plugging away. I kept focusing on what I learned and I kept dreaming. I thought I had it all under control. My health began to improve; the doctor was quite pleased with my accomplishment and, frankly, I felt pretty good about myself as well.

As of October, 2001, I was down 55 pounds and then I hit the wall! For four months I bounced up and down within 2 to 3 pounds.

I was on a huge plateau and nothing could get me off of it. And what did I do? You guessed it! I abandoned everything I learned; I forgot the dream; I said, "I told you it wouldn't work". And then I proved it. I ate like there was no tomorrow. I didn't care anymore. I gave up. I failed again! I started gaining weight twice as fast as I had lost it. The more depressed about it I became, the more I ate. By mid-2003, I had gained the 55 pounds plus another 50, and I was wearing a size 32 dress – a far cry from the size 12 that was in my thoughts just a few years before.

I was embarrassed, frustrated and depressed. My health was disintegrating rapidly. I could barely walk. I was convinced that each day was my last. My doctor had no idea what to do other than offer me anti-depressant pills to "help me get my mindset back in place to lose weight." I refused the pills.

My husband was so worried about me that he began to encourage me to see a surgeon about gastric bypass surgery. As bad as my health was, I just couldn't bring myself to do it. I did not do well with surgery and I knew that this was just a physical adjustment. The surgery wasn't the answer, it was my mind that was holding me back. My mind had to change before I could take on any plan to reduce my weight.

I continued out of control until September, 2003, when my whole life changed – literally!

After working in the same company for 20 years, I was "retired". The company had gone through many years of downturns and was finally bought out by another firm a few years earlier, but the downward spiral continued. Now, at age 56, I was out of a job for the first time in my life.

As part of my "package", I was included in an outplacement

*programme. On our first day we each had to get up in front of the group
and tell everyone who we were, where we had come from and what our
goals and fears were about searching for a new job. Not surprising, my
opening statement was, "I am 56 years old and morbidly obese. I will
never find a job regardless of my skills, my experience, my abilities."
The group was encouraging and didn't believe I would have a problem.
However, deep down, I knew that our society definitely was biased by an
individual's appearance.*

*When I went home that night, I talked to my husband, Stan,
about my fears, and we discussed all of our options. At that point,
I recalled that many years before I had drawn up a "life's plan", a
'summary' of my dreams and goals for the future. When I showed this
document to my husband he was amazed at what I had written. What
was surprising to him was the fact that many of my goals were his goals
(after 34 years of marriage, what did he expect?).*

*Using this document as the basis of our decisions about what we
would do going forward was the best thing that we did for ourselves.
We had time on our hands; I was given a great severance package which
would give me more than a year to step into my next phase of life. With
this in mind, we began to explore opportunities.*

*Because of my health problems – which included arthritis not
helped by the cold climate in New England – one of our other goals was
to live in a warmer area of the country. In mid-October, we took a trip
to Florida, checked out Orlando, visited home after home and found a
new community being developed in a perfect area for us. We signed the
contract to build our home and went back to New England to tell our*

family and to put our house up for sale. The house sold within 3 weeks and, by December 23, we moved into our new home! When we make a decision we don't mess around – we do it!

By the time we were in and settled I was physically exhausted. I had lost 14 pounds during the busy months planning and executing the move. But, by January I could not walk – just going to the local home improvement store was painful. I had to use electric carts to get around. When my family visited and we went to any of the amusement parks in the area, I had to rent a cart. There was no way I could manage to walk 5 or 6 hours – I could barely walk 5 or 6 minutes without needing to rest. My diabetes was out of control; I had high-blood pressure; my legs and feet were swollen all of the time.

My husband and I sat down and talked about our new life. We really liked the environment; we loved our new home; the weather was awesome and my arthritis was feeling better. But, unless I did something quickly, it was going to be a very short-lived adventure. If I continued down this path, I didn't expect to live to my next birthday.

So I did something radical – I called my tutor and 'confessed'. I asked him to tell me what I had done wrong. Why did I not succeed at my earlier attempt to diet? Why didn't it work for me? I told him that I felt like a failure and that if I was going to work for the company, I had to set an example.

His explanation about my failure was incredible. Basically, he told me that my goal was not properly set. I became obsessed with the numbers. When I didn't lose 2 pounds I got angry. I was sticking to my plan; I was as good as gold; I was doing everything I was supposed to do.

It was unacceptable for me to just lose half a pound in a week! It wasn't what I wanted.

He also told me that I was very hard on myself. I never congratulated myself for what I did accomplish. My thoughts were always that it wasn't good enough. I had to lose 110 pounds not 55. At this rate it would take me years to get to my goal. I beat myself up constantly. I never looked at what I had achieved, only how much more I had to go. I regained all the weight I had lost and more – the classic yo-yo.

I thought long and hard about what Andrew told me. He was right. Everything he said hit home. My first goal was "Blue Dress, Paris". Now I know that sounds silly to you, but I had learned that you have to have a visual connection to your goals, and you have to have an emotional connection as well. You need to picture yourself in a situation and then you have to feel it – let it get into your heart and mind. Once you find that picture and the feelings that go with it, use that as your goal.

When I had lost the 55 pounds, my husband and I had taken a trip to Paris. I wore a lovely blue dress that was soft, flowing, and feminine (even thought it was a size 20 dress, it was much smaller than anything I had fitted into in more than 30 years). We walked from our hotel, along the Seine River, and strolled past the cafes. The weather was balmy, the setting was perfect, and I felt great. This became my new goal: Blue Dress, Paris! I dug the dress out of the storage box, cleaned and pressed it and hung it in my closet where I could see it every time I walked in. I wrote my DayDream on index cards and left one on my desk, another in my handbag and another in the bathroom with my makeup. Everyday I would look at the cards, see the dress, and close my eyes and picture how I felt and looked when I wore my blue dress in Paris.

For me, by seeing my blue dress each day and reading the cards I had posted around the house, helped me create a pathway in my brain that was deeper and wider than the Grand Canyon. Once a pathway becomes larger than others, when faced with a decision you will take the path of least resistance – the larger bandwidth. Food was losing its control over me. When I was faced with a choice – a doughnut or a peach – my new pathway said, "My goal is Blue Dress, Paris – the doughnut won't get me there but the peach will." So I'd choose the peach!

From January to April, 2004, I started to lose weight again. With a weight management programme selected, my blue dress hanging in the closet, and my index cards at hand, I moved ahead. By December, 2004, I had lost another 76 pounds, and guess what? I fitted into my blue dress! Yahoo! I couldn't believe it. I thought about what I had accomplished and was quite pleased with myself. First goal accomplished.

I had lost a total of 97 pounds during the year. My health had improved dramatically. It had been six months since I needed to use an electric cart. I was walking without help and doing great. I did not suffer from shortness of breath. I could actually walk with my husband and keep up with him. When I started this adventure I was on five medications, now I was down to three. My diabetes was under control, my blood pressure was doing great and my feet were no longer swollen. Everyone told me that I looked healthy, strong, and younger (just what a woman wants to hear).

I wanted more! At this point, I was so happy that I could walk unassisted, but I decided that I needed to begin adding other forms of exercise. Since exercise was so foreign to me, I had to set a new goal and picture a new DayDream. I remembered how I felt as a child when I rode my bicycle. I loved it and would spend hours riding all around the neighbourhood with my friends, and often by myself, because I enjoyed it so much. I could see it; I could feel it.

However, there was an obstacle in my way. I needed to find a bicycle that I could ride that would not affect my right knee. It was arthritic; many years ago I had surgery on it; it never healed well nor felt right. It was weak and it had no flexibility. A standard bicycle just didn't do it – the downward motion of pedalling caused me pain! My husband is an avid shopper so I left the task to him to find something that would work. I wouldn't give up on my goal.

Finally, Stan found me the perfect bicycle. It was funky! The second I saw it I knew it was made for me! We went to the bike shop and the salesman took me out to the parking lot to try it out. The last time I had ridden a bicycle was more than 30 years ago. To brake on my last bike you just had to back pedal and you'd stop. I had never ridden a bike with gears and hand brakes. I didn't even know which was which. Fundamentally, this was a problem during my test ride. I got going and was doing great. I felt like a kid again – wind blowing in my hair; my knee wasn't hurting; sheer bliss and jubilation. Until I came to a slight downward incline and started picking up speed. I back pedalled to stop but nothing happened. Of course, you guessed it? I panicked and promptly fell off the bike.

As I was lying in the parking lot, totally embarrassed, my husband and the salesman came running up to me to see if I was okay. I got back up and took stock – everything was still where it was supposed to be. I asked them how to stop the thing and took the bike from their hands – if you could have seen their faces. They both said in unison, "You are going to get back on the bike again?" I just smiled at them and told them it was great. I loved it. They thought I was crazy, but I loved feeling like a kid again. I got back on the bike and drove around a bit more. Not only did I buy the bike but my husband bought one just like it.

When we got home, we rode our bikes around the neighbourhood. I could only go about a mile! Little by little I increased the time, distance and duration of our rides, until I got up to 12 miles. Amazing!

During 2005 I stuck with it, kept picturing my DayDreams, meeting each one of them with ease. I increased my exercise and ended up the year with a total weight loss of 157 pounds. I was just 8 pounds from my doctor's original weight goal for me. Then strange things started to happen - I hit the mother of all plateaus. During the first three months of the year, I managed to lose 2 whole pounds. Now I had six more to go! How hard could it be? It was the most torturous experience of my life.

I tried everything – I ate more, I ate less, I cut carbs, I ate more protein, added more fat, ate less fat, increased my water intake, and I increased my exercise – even joined a women's workout club and exercising three mornings a week. I was getting frustrated and angry. I was being as good as gold but I could not break the barrier. I bounced up and down within those six pounds for months!

Then my weight management instructor made the mistake of

saying to me, "Perhaps you should just go back to your doctor and get a note saying that the weight you are at now is your goal – your body is happy where it is?" That really did it – I got angry. I had a dream and I was going to reach it without compromise. I didn't care if my body was happy, I was not!

After a few weeks of this, suddenly my mind became very clear – I needed to shock my body, it had become complacent. So I stayed on my weight management plan for four days and cut back my food intake significantly for three days. Result – the first week I lost four pounds – two pounds from goal! So I tried it again the next week and, when I went to weigh in, I sneaked a peak before I went to my class. My scale at home showed that I was lower than my goal weight – I prayed that, during the next hour, I wouldn't gain a pound! Lo and behold, when I weighed in, I had done it! I was finally below my goal weight.

It has taken me 36.5 years to get here. I have lost a total of 165 pounds to date. I've met the doctor's goal and my health is incredible. I am no longer taking any medications at all. I can walk; I can ride a bicycle; I can work out in a gym. I chase our grandson around the house.

I now feel as though I can live to be at least 95 (I'll review my feelings at that time). Food no longer controls me. I still enjoying eating and cooking but I have learned about making choices. I never knew how many people I had on my team! Family and friends have been such a support to me. I could never have done it without their help. And, I think I have taught them a few things along the way. I certainly hope I inspired them in some way.

*Recently, my husband found a picture of me in June, 2003 (6
months before I started dieting). I was at my highest weight. It is
a visible testament to how far I have come. I don't really care what
my weight number is. What is important is that I look, act, and feel
different. My life has totally changed and I can't wait to see what the
future has in store.*

Jan's story highlights that dreams can take time, and
shows that resilience is important. As soon as she focused on
the problems and the tasks, she fell short. She demonstrates
that when her eye was on her dream she achieved.

Think of times when you have focused on the tasks behind
a goal and allowed the sheer enormity of them to de-motivate
you. For example; thinking about how much revising you have
to do for an exam can detract from your inspirational vision of
celebrating success on graduation day. Keep the DayDream
in mind and you will move to fulfil the important and necessary
tasks to get there. The vision drives you to plan, to revise, to
work and sacrifice time and effort to get you there.

What can you relate to in Jan's story? What can you learn
from it?

RuleEleven
The
Prescription

11

Visualise them at least 3 times a day!

 "Repetition, in itself breeds the further probability of repetition."
TONY BUZAN

One final time…remember the equation:

$$I \times F = B$$

OK, maybe I should repeat it a few more times just for good measure.

$$I \times F = B \quad I \times F = B$$

$$I \times F = B \quad I \times F = B$$

$$I \times F = B \quad I \times F = B$$

$$I \times F = B \quad I \times F = B$$

*Intensity x **F**requency = **B**andwidth*

The more frequently that you picture your dream, the more you think about your vision, the stronger it will become. This is not just anecdotal. It has been proven that the more times a 'mental event' takes place, the less resistance exists towards it happening again. As I have already mentioned, this is quite physical and quite literal. A thought, remember, is a physical thing in your brain – electricity firing between two or more brain cells, transferring chemicals that drive your emotions and actions.

The more we think a particular thought, the stronger the pathway between those brain cells and the stronger the signal to our body to act upon that thought. Whether that thought is good or bad for us, we will act according to our strongest pathways. Electricity will inevitably travel along the paths of least resistance. If you get the previous rules correct then you stand a great chance of building the right pathways. The more you picture your true DayDream, the more you are physically building your pathway to achieve the goal behind it. Once is better than not at all. Three times is better than twice. When you really start to build towards your dream, you won't be able to resist thinking about it all day!

 "It is the repetition…that leads to belief. And once that belief becomes a deep conviction, things begin to happen"
MUHAMMAD ALI

The inventor and Godfather of Horse Whispering is an

amazing man called Monty Roberts. Monty learnt at an early age that to get what you want, you have to have vision. At the age of thirteen, a son of a horse trainer, he went to the deserts of Nevada from his home in California and, whilst there, he studied wild mustangs in their natural habitat.

Monty observed their patterns of behaviour and learnt to translate that into a technique for communicating with animals. A real life Doctor Dolittle! The language is called Equus and involves observation, body movements, positioning and sounds.

His father was a hard man and Monty's treatment as a child was tough to say the least. His newfound methodology of communication was seen as a challenge to his father's way and was treated as such, yet Monty wouldn't give up.

Now Monty is a hugely successful horse trainer, using his methods of cooperation, as opposed to domination, to improve behaviourally challenged horses. He travels the world, is perhaps the most famous name in horse training today, and his methods are seen as 'The Way it Should Be Done'.

Monty's methods of building trust and respect with his 'patients' sit well with research into the most effective ways to develop businesses. I've been to spend time with Monty and his team, and have learnt huge amounts in terms of leadership, communication and influence.

His messages are truly amazing.

I had the pleasure of attending a session Monty was running in the UK a couple of years ago. The nature of these sessions is for Monty to take 4 or 5 troubled horses and work with them in front of a large audience, demonstrating his methods of building trust and creating rapport with his 'student'. The idea is that 2000 horse enthusiasts take those methods and that knowledge away with them to use back at the stable.

What most people don't see is the pre-show audition. Monty wants to make sure that the audience is entertained and that they learn something useful, so he 'auditions' horses for their part in the evening's proceedings. At no point does he come into contact with the horses he will work with later. All he does is observe them and speak with the owner, to get a feel for the problems. They can range from refusing to be saddled, to refusing to climb aboard a horse box, to freaking out any time cattle come near!

Monty looks for a nice mix that will work as a show. Some horses are therefore refused but that doesn't make them any less appropriate for work. Monty will often spend time with the 'rejects' in order to help owners gain some ground. Sometimes, he is forced to help just to get the horse into its box to travel home!

Stood in the ring with Monty, I had the pleasure of watching him work at close hand. He went through a process called 'Join Up', where he metaphorically asks the horse to 'join up' with him. Once the horse accepts the invitation, Monty knows that he is now the boss! With this foundation of trust built, he can now 'talk' the horse into getting into the lorry for itself, rather than forcing it to. He managed to do this so well that the horse was eventually pulling Monty onto the truck with him!

The few people that attended, were in awe of the achievement, and were happy to sit back and enjoy the moment and the success. Not Monty. He then proceeded to repeat the process four or five times, each time teaching the horse to wait for guidance from him, rather than roughly pushing him on board. He justified this extra effort for both him and horse by telling everyone that if the horse pushed the owner on board, who weighed half that of Monty's bodyweight, it could be potentially dangerous. He wanted the horse to form a new habit, and by repeating the process just a few times, that's exactly what Monty helped the horse to do. He turned to me and said:

 **"I have learned in my life that repetition, when you are doing the right thing, is your best friend. Repetition when you are doing the wrong thing is your worst enemy."**

MONTY ROBERTS, THE REAL LIFE HORSE WHISPERER

TopTips

- Visualise your DayDreams at least 3 times a day
- Keep them on your person to remind you
- Place them in appropriate locations where you cannot avoid them

"I have learned in my life that repetition, when you are doing the right thing, is your best friend. Repetition when you are doing the wrong thing is your worst enemy."

MONTY ROBERTS, THE REAL LIFE HORSE WHISPERER

DayDreaming

- **Simple premise**
- **Simple rules**
- **Simple outcomes**

You now have all you need to put your goals into a format that will help you bring them to life – both metaphorically and literally.

Remember the rules:

Keep it personal
There is no time like the present
The devil is in the detail
Give yourself goose bumps
Don't look now but…
Nothing compares to you
You can't kid a kidder
A need to know basis
Walk the tightrope
The pen is mightier…
The prescription

What I have written about in this book is at work in you 24 hours a day. Now you know how to use it more often and to use it better.

Remember the quote from the very beginning of this book…

"All men dream, but not equally. Those who dream by night in the dusty recesses of their minds wake in the day to find that it was vanity: but the dreamers of the day are dangerous men, for they may act their dreams with open eyes, to make it possible."

T.E.LAWRENCE, THE SEVEN PILLARS OF WISDOM

As T.E. Lawrence explained, we spend our lives doing what we thought was DayDreaming, only to find that it was fantasy. However, we have all truly DayDreamed in the past, and we can do it again in the future.

DayDreaming:
Redefine the word, redefine your goals,
and redefine your life.

It is May 1st 2009. I am sat with my little girl Eve in my arms. The fire roars, popping and crackling and candles burn on the mantelpiece casting a warm glow over the room as music plays over the stereo. I lean back into the couch and hear the squeaking and creaking of the leather under my body. I turn to Laurie as she puts down the book: My book. She hands me a glass of champagne and pours one for herself. We chink glasses and smile about how amazing the last year has been since our little miracle was born. To think this was just a pile of pages at that point. We toast my first book – written and published. I am in print, 2 years after setting out to be.

I am a true DayDreamer.

**The following books provided inspiration for this one...
Without them, and many others for that matter, this book
(along with many others in this field) would not exist.**

Adrian Gilpin
UNSTOPPABLE PEOPLE

A superb book, distilling the entire self help section of the bookstore into one great read.

Ellen Macarthur
TAKING ON THE WORLD

A fantastic story of courage and determination. Ellen shows that if you dream well enough, you can make it happen.

Gordon Ramsey
HUMBLE PIE

Some people don't identify with Gordon Ramsey. I think he is hugely inspirational. He is a man who has worked hard to achieve his dreams.

Pat Mesiti
WAKE UP AND DREAM

A great book about the power of personal visions.

Christopher Reeve
STILL ME

One of my favourite books, written by a true life super hero. Reeve is prepared to believe so strongly in his vision that simply by reading about it, you are prepared to believe with him.

James Cracknell and Ben Fogle
THE CROSSING

An incredible feat, and an amazing story. How they did it, only they know.

Tony Buzan
THE MIND MAPPING BOOK

A fantastic encyclopaedia about how to get the best from the grey matter in your skull.

Damian Hughes
LIQUID THINKING

Damian is a good friend of mine and he writes superb books: Damian... I finally got there!

Tim Moore
FRENCH REVOLUTIONS

Inspired Wayne to ride the Tour de France route. Enough said.

John Medina
BRAIN RULES

Medina takes a huge subject and turns it into something understandable and engaging.

Monty Roberts
THE REAL LIFE HORSE WHISPERER

An amazing story about an amazing man with an amazing purpose and talent. Monty rules.

Lance Armstrong
IT'S NOT ABOUT THE BIKE

Armstrong's first book is riveting from start to finish. You ride every inch of the way with him.

Malcolm Gladwell
BLINK

A fascinating insight into the mind and our gut reactions, looking at how powerful our filter is.

W Clement Stone
THE SUCCESS SYSTEM THAT NEVER FAILS

The Godfather of positive thinking, Stone had many of the answers before we had the proof.

Susan Greenfield
THE PRIVATE LIFE OF THE BRAIN

A great book taking readers deeper into the brain and its workings.

National Geographic
JUNE 1995

Quiet Miracles of the Brain. The article that started it all off! A great piece written in an engaging style. It set the standard for teaching laymen about the brain.

Books

TO THE DAYDREAMERS WHO MADE IT IN:

WAYNE, MIKE, NICK, NEIL AND JAN

Your stories are the bread and butter of this book. Without you there would be nothing to write about. Thanks for sharing a little bit of you with the world.

TO THE DAYDREAMERS THAT DIDN'T MAKE IT IN:

ALAN, DAVE, ANNE, JANINE, RUTH AND SCOTT

Your stories are just as important and significant. They will form the basis of the next book. Thanks for being patient!

TO MY FRIENDS AT ADVANCE.

Without you this book wouldn't exist. YOU gave me the start and the platform. Thanks for the chance to aim for greatness and for making everyday an absolute pleasure. Keep changing people's lives.

TO MELANIE

You tirelessly typed up the interviews that form the backbone of the book – brilliant. Thanks for smiling through the requests!

TO DARCENIA

You added correctness to the research and asked the right questions of the right people on my behalf. Thanks for making this official.

TO KARLOS THE ILLUSTRATOR!

I can't wait to see your name in lights on a Disney movie. Thanks for your time and effort and amazing artistic talent.

TO PAUL AT DESIGNLEFT

Designer supreme – what an amazing job you did of bringing the words to life. It's everything I dreamed of and more.

TO JACQUI, HEATHER AND DANIEL

My unofficial editors! Thank you for picking up the detail on my behalf and making so many great suggestions. It is appreciated.

TO SUZY AND EMMA AT PEPPERMINT PR

Thankyou for all your help. Not least with this little project!

TO ALL MY FRIENDS

You know who you are. There are too many of you to mention and I don't want to leave any of you out. You are very important to me. Best play safe then and just say thanks to you all.

TO ALL OF MY FAMILY, YOUNG AND OLD, NEAR AND FAR

Especially though to Debbie, "you are the real golden child", and Mandy, "don't act like you're not impressed!"

TO MY MUM 'N DAD

You are my heroes, always there for me, unconditionally. Mum, you got me into this so a big part of this book is for you. Who would have thought I would have beaten you to it? Dad, how do you put up with me? Hope this makes up for failing to become an F1 driver.

TO EVE AND HENRY

Thanks for being our little miracles. You are the proof that DayDreams really do come true. I can't wait to watch you achieving all your DayDreams in life.

TO LAURIE

Thanks for making everyday a pleasure. Thanks for giving me the ultimate gift. This book is for you; it's all for you. I will love you always.

...a better world

Simon Clarkson was born and raised in Lancashire. After studying Economics at Leeds University, he worked in Investment Banking based in London. In 2002 he moved back to the North West. After working in the personal and organisational development industry for around 10 years, Simon now owns and runs Think Works – a world class performance enhancement training company. He is married to Laurie and they have a two children, Eve and Henry. They live near the seaside in Lytham St Annes. This is Simon's first book.

Find out more about the author and Think Works at www.thinkworks.org.uk.
A contribution from the proceeds of this book will go to Derian House Children's Hospice.